Presented to

Alex Roberts

By

Brendan McIntyre

On the Occasion of

Highfield S.S. Award.

Date

January 24, 2010.

"Seek and ye shall
find."

Bible Answers
for
STUDENTS

BARBOUR
PUBLISHING

Published by Barbour Publishing, Inc., P.O. Box 719, Uhrichsville, Ohio 44683, www.barbourbooks.com

Our mission is to publish and distribute inspirational products offering exceptional value and biblical encouragement to the masses.

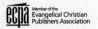
Member of the
Evangelical Christian
Publishers Association

Printed in the United States of America.

INTRODUCTION

As a student, you've got enough stresses in life—you may be worried about that upcoming school event or your next exam. When you're facing so much at once, where do you turn for answers?

That's what *Bible Answers for Students* is all about. This collection of scriptures will sharpen your focus on the real issues of life—spiritual matters of the deepest importance. You'll find forty-one relevant topics, each packed with God's ultimate truth. Brief introductions and thought-provoking quotations enhance each section, making this a book to refer to for years to come.

Of course, no book should substitute for daily Bible reading and study. We hope *Bible Answers for Students* will always point you toward the one Book that is truth—the Bible. With God's Word as your guide, you can't go wrong in the life ahead!

Contents

ADVERSITY

The LORD also will be a refuge for the oppressed, a refuge in times of trouble. And those who know Your name will put their trust in You; for You, LORD, have not forsaken those who seek You.

PSALM 9:9–10 NKJV

For even Christ did not please himself but, as it is written: "The insults of those who insult you have fallen on me." For everything that was written in the past was written to teach us, so that through endurance and the encouragement of the Scriptures we might have hope.

ROMANS 15:3–4 NIV

Are any of you suffering hardships? You should pray. Are any of you happy? You should sing praises.

JAMES 5:13 NLT

Even though I walk through the valley of the shadow of death, I fear no evil, for You are with me; Your rod and Your staff, they comfort me.

PSALM 23:4 NASB

Casting all your care upon Him, for He cares for you.

1 PETER 5:7 NKJV

"When you pass through the waters, I will be with you; and through the rivers, they will not overflow you. When you walk through the fire, you will not be scorched, nor will the flame burn you."

ISAIAH 43:2 NASB

For the Lord will not reject forever, for if He causes grief, then He will have compassion according to His abundant lovingkindness.

LAMENTATIONS 3:31–32 NASB

But rejoice to the extent that you partake of Christ's sufferings, that when His glory is revealed, you may also be glad with exceeding joy.

1 PETER 4:13 NKJV

If you are reproached for the name of Christ, blessed are you, for the Spirit of glory and of God rests upon you. On their part He is blasphemed, but on your part He is glorified.

1 PETER 4:14 NKJV

Record my lament; list my tears on your scroll—are they not in your record? Then my enemies will turn back when I call for help. By this I will know that God is for me.

PSALM 56:8–9 NIV

For as the sufferings of Christ abound in us, so our consolation also aboundeth by Christ. And whether we be afflicted, it is for your consolation and salvation, which is effectual in the enduring of the same sufferings which we also suffer: or whether we be comforted, it is for your consolation and salvation. And our hope of you is stedfast, knowing, that as ye are partakers of the sufferings, so shall ye be also of the consolation.

2 CORINTHIANS 1:5–7 KJV

"Blessed are those who mourn, for they shall be comforted."

MATTHEW 5:4 NKJV

He will swallow up death forever! The Sovereign LORD will wipe away all tears. He will remove forever all insults and mockery against his land and people. The LORD has spoken!

ISAIAH 25:8 NLT

"Do not fear any of those things which you are about to suffer. Indeed, the devil is about to throw some of you into prison, that you may be tested, and you will have tribulation ten days. Be faithful until death, and I will give you the crown of life."

REVELATION 2:10 NKJV

The Lord is good, a stronghold in the day of trouble; and He knows those who trust in Him.

NAHUM 1:7 NKJV

"Come to Me, all you who labor and are heavy laden, and I will give you rest. Take My yoke upon you and learn from Me, for I am gentle and lowly in heart, and you will find rest for your souls. For My yoke is easy and My burden is light."

MATTHEW 11:28–30 NKJV

For this finds favor, if for the sake of conscience toward God a person bears up under sorrows when suffering unjustly. For what credit is there if, when you sin and are harshly treated, you endure it with patience? But if when you do what is right and suffer for it you patiently endure it, this finds favor with God. For you have been called for this purpose, since Christ also suffered for you, leaving you an example for you to follow in His steps, WHO COMMITTED NO SIN, NOR WAS ANY DECEIT FOUND IN HIS MOUTH; and while being reviled, He did not revile in return; while suffering, He uttered no threats, but kept entrusting Himself to Him who judges righteously.

1 PETER 2:19–23 NASB

For our light affliction, which is but for a moment, worketh for us a far more exceeding and eternal weight of glory.

2 CORINTHIANS 4:17 KJV

And lest I should be exalted above measure through the abundance of the revelations, there was given to me a thorn in the flesh, the messenger of Satan to buffet me, lest I should be exalted above measure. For this thing I besought the Lord thrice, that it might depart from me. And he said unto me, My grace is sufficient for thee: for my strength is made perfect in weakness. Most gladly therefore will I rather glory in my infirmities, that the power of Christ may rest upon me.

2 CORINTHIANS 12:7–9 KJV

Weeping may remain for a night, but rejoicing comes in the morning.

PSALM 30:5 NIV

"Blessed are you who hunger now, for you shall be satisfied. Blessed are you who weep now, for you shall laugh. Blessed are you when men hate you, and ostracize you, and insult you, and scorn your name as evil, for the sake of the Son of Man. Be glad in that day and leap for joy, for behold, your reward is great in heaven. For in the same way their fathers used to treat the prophets."

LUKE 6:21–23 NASB

The righteous cry out, and the LORD hears, and delivers them out of all their troubles.

PSALM 34:17 NKJV

"I have told you all this so that you may have peace in me. Here on earth you will have many trials and sorrows. But take heart, because I have overcome the world."

JOHN 16:33 NLT

In this you greatly rejoice, even though now for a little while, if necessary, you have been distressed by various trials, so that the proof of your faith, being more precious than gold which is perishable, even though tested by fire, may be found to result in praise and glory and honor at the revelation of Jesus Christ.

1 PETER 1:6–7 NASB

After you have suffered for a little while, the God of all grace, who called you to His eternal glory in Christ, will Himself perfect, confirm, strengthen and establish you.

1 PETER 5:10 NASB

Blessed is the man who endures temptation; for when he has been approved, he will receive the crown of life which the Lord has promised to those who love Him.

JAMES 1:12 NKJV

For I consider that the sufferings of this present time are not worthy to be compared with the glory that is to be revealed to us.

ROMANS 8:18 NASB

Rejoicing in hope, persevering in tribulation, devoted to prayer. . .

ROMANS 12:12 NASB

ANGER

My dear brothers, take note of this: Everyone should be quick to listen, slow to speak and slow to become angry, for man's anger does not bring about the righteous life that God desires.

JAMES 1:19-20 NIV

Do not associate with a man given to anger; or go with a hot-tempered man, or you will learn his ways and find a snare for yourself.

PROVERBS 22:24–25 NASB

Control your temper, for anger labels you a fool.

ECCLESIASTES 7:9 NLT

The discretion of a man makes him slow to anger, and his glory is to overlook a transgression.

PROVERBS 19:11 NKJV

A fool's wrath is presently known: but a prudent man covereth shame.

PROVERBS 12:16 KJV

"For wrath kills a foolish man, and envy slays a simple one."

JOB 5:2 NKJV

Do all things without grumbling or disputing.

PHILIPPIANS 2:14 NASB

BE ANGRY, AND yet DO NOT SIN; do not let the sun go down on your anger, and do not give the devil an opportunity. . . . Let all bitterness and wrath and anger and clamor and slander be put away from you, along with all malice.

EPHESIANS 4:26–27, 31 NASB

"But I say to you that whoever is angry with his brother without a cause shall be in danger of the judgment. And whoever says to his brother, 'Raca!' shall be in danger of the council. But whoever says, 'You fool!' shall be in danger of hell fire."

MATTHEW 5:22 NKJV

A gentle answer turns away wrath, but a harsh word stirs up anger. . . . A hot-tempered man stirs up strife, but the slow to anger calms a dispute.

PROVERBS 15:1, 18 NASB

Starting a quarrel is like breaching a dam; so drop the matter before a dispute breaks out.

PROVERBS 17:14 NIV

Dear friends, never take revenge. Leave that to the righteous anger of God. For the Scriptures say, "I will take revenge; I will pay them back," says the LORD.

ROMANS 12:19 NLT

A man of great wrath will suffer punishment; for if you rescue him, you will have to do it again.

PROVERBS 19:19 NKJV

Cease from anger and forsake wrath; do not fret; it leads only to evildoing.

PSALM 37:8 NASB

He that is soon angry dealeth foolishly. . . . He that is slow to wrath is of great understanding: but he that is hasty of spirit exalteth folly.

PROVERBS 14:17, 29 KJV

But now you yourselves are to put off all these: anger, wrath, malice, blasphemy, filthy language out of your mouth.

COLOSSIANS 3:8 NKJV

COMFORT

"And I will pray the Father, and He will give you another Helper, that He may abide with you forever."

JOHN 14:16 NKJV

Yea, though I walk through the valley of the shadow of death, I will fear no evil: for thou art with me; thy rod and thy staff they comfort me.

PSALM 23:4 KJV

"He will wipe every tear from their eyes. There will be no more death or mourning or crying or pain, for the old order of things has passed away."

REVELATION 21:4 NIV

The Lord GOD will wipe away tears from all faces.

ISAIAH 25:8 NKJV

For the Lord himself shall descend from heaven with a shout, with the voice of the archangel, and with the trump of God: and the dead in Christ shall rise first: Then we which are alive and remain shall be caught up together with them in the clouds, to meet the Lord in the air: and so shall we ever be with the Lord. Wherefore comfort one another with these words.

1 THESSALONIANS 4:16–18 KJV

Cast all your anxiety on him because he cares for you.

1 PETER 5:7 NIV

"Comfort, O comfort My people," says your God.

ISAIAH 40:1 NASB

When doubts filled my mind, your comfort gave me renewed hope and cheer.

PSALM 94:19 NLT

Blessed are they that mourn: for they shall be comforted.

MATTHEW 5:4 KJV

Thou shalt increase my greatness, and comfort me on every side.

PSALM 71:21 KJV

"I am with you always, even to the end of the age."

MATTHEW 28:20 NLT

"Come to me, all you who are weary and burdened, and I will give you rest."

MATTHEW 11:28 NIV

I will not leave you comfortless: I will come to you.

JOHN 14:18 KJV

I remembered thy judgments of old, O LORD; and have comforted myself.

PSALM 119:52 KJV

"As one whom his mother comforts, so I will comfort you."

ISAIAH 66:13 NASB

All praise to God, the Father of our Lord Jesus Christ. God is our merciful Father and the source of all comfort. He comforts us in all our troubles so that we can comfort others. When they are troubled, we will be able to give them the same comfort God has given us. For the more we suffer for Christ, the more God will shower us with his comfort through Christ.

2 CORINTHIANS 1:3–5 NLT

Be perfect, be of good comfort, be of one mind, live in peace; and the God of love and peace shall be with you.

2 CORINTHIANS 13:11 KJV

Come near to God and he will come near to you.

JAMES 4:8 NIV

CONVERSATION

When words are many, sin is not absent, but he who holds his tongue is wise.

PROVERBS 10:19 NIV

"A good man out of the good treasure of his heart brings forth good things, and an evil man out of the evil treasure brings forth evil things. But I say to you that for every idle word men may speak, they will give account of it in the day of judgment. For by your words you will be justified, and by your words you will be condemned."

MATTHEW 12:35–37 NKJV

Do not speak evil of one another, brethren. He who speaks evil of a brother and judges his brother, speaks evil of the law and judges the law. But if you judge the law, you are not a doer of the law but a judge.

JAMES 4:11 NKJV

A man has joy in an apt answer, and how delightful is a timely word!

PROVERBS 15:23 NASB

But now ye also put off all these; anger, wrath, malice, blasphemy, filthy communication out of your mouth.

COLOSSIANS 3:8 KJV

For the Scriptures say, "If you want to enjoy life and see many happy days, keep your tongue from speaking evil and your lips from telling lies."

1 PETER 3:10 NLT

Let your speech always be with grace, as though seasoned with salt, so that you will know how you should respond to each person.

COLOSSIANS 4:6 NASB

If anyone thinks himself to be religious, and yet does not bridle his tongue but deceives his own heart, this man's religion is worthless.

JAMES 1:26 NASB

Let no corrupt word proceed out of your mouth, but what is good for necessary edification, that it may impart grace to the hearers.

EPHESIANS 4:29 NKJV

"When they bring you before the synagogues and the rulers and the authorities, do not worry about how or what you are to speak in your defense, or what you are to say; for the Holy Spirit will teach you in that very hour what you ought to say."

LUKE 12:11–12 NASB

I said, "I will watch my ways and keep my tongue from sin; I will put a muzzle on my mouth as long as the wicked are in my presence."

PSALM 39:1 NIV

For we all stumble in many ways. If anyone does not stumble in what he says, he is a perfect man, able to bridle the whole body as well. Now if we put the bits into the horses' mouths so that they will obey us, we direct their entire body as well. Look at the ships also, though they are so great and are driven by strong winds, are still directed by a very small rudder wherever the inclination of the pilot desires. So also the tongue is a small part of the body, and yet it boasts of great things. See how great a forest is set aflame by such a small fire! And the tongue is a fire, the very world of iniquity; the tongue is set among our members as that which defiles the entire body, and sets on fire the course of our life, and is set on fire by hell. For every species of beasts and birds, of reptiles and creatures of the sea, is tamed and has been tamed by the human race. But no one can tame the tongue; it is a restless evil and full of deadly poison. With it we bless our Lord and Father, and with it we curse men, who have been made in the likeness of God; from the same mouth come both blessing and cursing. My brethren, these things ought not to be this way.

JAMES 3:2–10 NASB

He who restrains his words has knowledge, and he who has a cool spirit is a man of understanding.

PROVERBS 17:27 NASB

Set a watch, O LORD, before my mouth; keep the door of my lips.

PSALM 141:3 KJV

A fool vents all his feelings, but a wise man holds them back.

PROVERBS 29:11 NKJV

He who guards his mouth and his tongue keeps himself from calamity.

PROVERBS 21:23 NIV

Do you see a man hasty in his words? There is more hope for a fool than for him.

PROVERBS 29:20 NKJV

COUNSEL

The way of a fool is right in his own eyes, but a wise man is he who listens to counsel.

PROVERBS 12:15 NASB

Then Jehoshaphat added, "But first let's find out what the LORD says."

1 KINGS 22:5 NLT

Listen to counsel and accept discipline, that you may be wise the rest of your days.

PROVERBS 19:20 NASB

For unto us a Child is born, unto us a Son is given; and the government will be upon His shoulder. And His name will be called Wonderful, Counselor.

ISAIAH 9:6 NKJV

Howbeit when he, the Spirit of truth, is come, he will guide you into all truth: for he shall not speak of himself; but whatsoever he shall hear, that shall he speak: and he will shew you things to come.

JOHN 16:13 KJV

All your children shall be taught by the LORD, and great shall be the peace of your children.

ISAIAH 54:13 NKJV

All discipline for the moment seems not to be joyful, but sorrowful; yet to those who have been trained by it, afterwards it yields the peaceful fruit of righteousness.

HEBREWS 12:11 NASB

Instruct a wise man and he will be wiser still; teach a righteous man and he will add to his learning.

PROVERBS 9:9 NIV

Brethren, if a man is overtaken in any trespass, you who are spiritual restore such a one in a spirit of gentleness, considering yourself lest you also be tempted.

GALATIANS 6:1 NKJV

"With Him are wisdom and strength, He has counsel and understanding."

JOB 12:13 NKJV

Gently instruct those who oppose the truth. Perhaps God will change those people's hearts, and they will learn the truth.

2 TIMOTHY 2:25 NLT

Oil and perfume make the heart glad, so a man's counsel is sweet to his friend.

PROVERBS 27:9 NASB

I will instruct thee and teach thee in the way which thou shalt go: I will guide thee with mine eye.

PSALM 32:8 KJV

"And those of the people who understand shall instruct many."

DANIEL 11:33 NKJV

Where there is no guidance the people fall, but in abundance of counselors there is victory.

PROVERBS 11:14 NASB

The Spirit of the LORD will rest on him—the Spirit of wisdom and of understanding, the Spirit of counsel and of power, the Spirit of knowledge and of the fear of the LORD.

ISAIAH 11:2 NIV

Blessed is the man who walks not in the counsel of the ungodly, nor stands in the path of sinners, nor sits in the seat of the scornful.

PSALM 1:1 NKJV

Without consultation, plans are frustrated, but with many counselors they succeed.

PROVERBS 15:22 NASB

The LORD of Heaven's Armies is a wonderful teacher, and he gives the farmer great wisdom.

ISAIAH 28:29 NLT

You will guide me with Your counsel, and afterward receive me to glory.

PSALM 73:24 NKJV

A wise man will hear and increase in learning, and a man of understanding will acquire wise counsel.

PROVERBS 1:5 NASB

COURAGE

So that we may boldly say, The Lord is my helper, and I will not fear what man shall do unto me.

HEBREWS 13:6 KJV

For God has not given us a spirit of fear, but of power and of love and of a sound mind.

2 TIMOTHY 1:7 NKJV

By this, love is perfected with us, so that we may have confidence in the day of judgment; because as He is, so also are we in this world.

1 JOHN 4:17 NASB

We have boldness and access with confidence through faith in Him.

EPHESIANS 3:12 NKJV

In the fear of the LORD there is strong confidence, and His children will have a place of refuge.

PROVERBS 14:26 NKJV

We have confidence to enter the holy place by the blood of Jesus.

HEBREWS 10:19 NASB

For the LORD will be your confidence and will keep your foot from being caught.

PROVERBS 3:26 NASB

Be brave, be strong.

1 CORINTHIANS 16:13 NKJV

And now, dear children, remain in fellowship with Christ so that when he returns, you will be full of courage and not shrink back from him in shame.

1 JOHN 2:28 NLT

Whatever happens, conduct yourselves in a manner worthy of the gospel of Christ. Then, whether I come and see you or only hear about you in my absence, I will know that you stand firm in one spirit, contending as one man for the faith of the gospel without being frightened in any way by those who oppose you. This is a sign to them that they will be destroyed, but that you will be saved—and that by God.

PHILIPPIANS 1:27–28 NIV

And thou, son of man, be not afraid of them, neither be afraid of their words, though briers and thorns be with thee, and thou dost dwell among scorpions: be not afraid of their words, nor be dismayed at their looks, though they be a rebellious house.

EZEKIEL 2:6 KJV

Therefore let us draw near with confidence to the throne of grace, so that we may receive mercy and find grace to help in time of need.

HEBREWS 4:16 NASB

Dear friends, if our hearts do not condemn us, we have confidence before God.

1 JOHN 3:21 NIV

The wicked flee when no one pursues, but the righteous are bold as a lion.

PROVERBS 28:1 NKJV

Be strong and let your heart take courage, all you who hope in the LORD.

PSALM 31:24 NASB

"By standing firm, you will win your souls."

LUKE 21:19 NLT

I can do all things through Christ who strengthens me.

PHILIPPIANS 4:13 NKJV

DISCIPLINE

"Thus you are to know in your heart that the LORD your God was disciplining you just as a man disciplines his son."

DEUTERONOMY 8:5 NASB

But when we are judged, we are chastened of the Lord, that we should not be condemned with the world.

1 CORINTHIANS 11:32 KJV

He who keeps instruction is in the way of life, but he who refuses correction goes astray.

PROVERBS 10:17 NKJV

"Behold, how happy is the man whom God reproves, so do not despise the discipline of the Almighty. For He inflicts pain, and gives relief; He wounds, and His hands also heal."

JOB 5:17–18 NASB

And you have forgotten that word of encouragement that addresses you as sons: "My son, do not make light of the Lord's discipline, and do not lose heart when he rebukes you, because the Lord disciplines those he loves, and he punishes everyone he accepts as a son." Endure hardship as discipline; God is treating you as sons. For what son is not disciplined by his father? If you are not disciplined (and everyone undergoes discipline), then you are illegitimate children and not true sons. Moreover, we have all had human fathers who disciplined us and we respected them for it. How much more should we submit to the Father of our spirits and live! Our fathers disciplined us for a little while as they thought best; but God disciplines us for our good, that we may share in his holiness. No discipline seems pleasant at the time, but painful. Later on, however, it produces a harvest of righteousness and peace for those who have been trained by it.

HEBREWS 12:5–11 NIV

The fear of the LORD is the beginning of knowledge, but fools despise wisdom and instruction.

PROVERBS 1:7 NKJV

He who chastens the nations, will He not rebuke, even He who teaches man knowledge?

PSALM 94:10 NASB

Blessed is the man whom You chasten, O LORD, and whom You teach out of Your law; that You may grant him relief from the days of adversity, until a pit is dug for the wicked.

PSALM 94:12–13 NASB

For their command is a lamp and their instruction a light; their corrective discipline is the way to life.

PROVERBS 6:23 NLT

"As many as I love, I rebuke and chasten. Therefore be zealous and repent."

REVELATION 3:19 NKJV

For whom the LORD loveth he correcteth; even as a father the son in whom he delighteth.

PROVERBS 3:12 KJV

ENCOURAGEMENT

So then, brethren, stand firm and hold to the traditions which you were taught, whether by word of mouth or by letter from us. Now may our Lord Jesus Christ Himself and God our Father, who has loved us and given us eternal comfort and good hope by grace, comfort and strengthen your hearts in every good work and word.

2 THESSALONIANS 2:15–17 NASB

Pure and undefiled religion before God and the Father is this: to visit orphans and widows in their trouble, and to keep oneself unspotted from the world.

JAMES 1:27 NKJV

Now the God of patience and consolation grant you to be likeminded one toward another according to Christ Jesus.

ROMANS 15:5 KJV

If we are distressed, it is for your comfort and salvation; if we are comforted, it is for your comfort, which produces in you patient endurance of the same sufferings we suffer.

2 CORINTHIANS 1:6 NIV

Therefore encourage one another and build up one another, just as you also are doing.

1 THESSALONIANS 5:11 NASB

The light of the eyes rejoices the heart, and a good report makes the bones healthy.

PROVERBS 15:30 NKJV

Don't look out only for your own interests, but take an interest in others, too.

PHILIPPIANS 2:4 NLT

He gives power to the weak, and to those who have no might He increases strength.

ISAIAH 40:29 NKJV

Little children, let us not love with word or with tongue, but in deed and truth.

1 JOHN 3:18 NASB

Bear one another's burdens, and so fulfill the law of Christ.

GALATIANS 6:2 NKJV

ETERNAL LIFE

But now that you have been set free from sin and have become slaves to God, the benefit you reap leads to holiness, and the result is eternal life. For the wages of sin is death, but the gift of God is eternal life in Christ Jesus our Lord.

ROMANS 6:22–23 NIV

"Do not work for the food which perishes, but for the food which endures to eternal life, which the Son of Man will give to you, for on Him the Father, God, has set His seal."

JOHN 6:27 NASB

"And everyone who has left houses or brothers or sisters or father or mother or children or fields for my sake will receive a hundred times as much and will inherit eternal life."

MATTHEW 19:29 NIV

For the one who sows to his own flesh will from the flesh reap corruption, but the one who sows to the Spirit will from the Spirit reap eternal life.

GALATIANS 6:8 NASB

The Spirit of God, who raised Jesus from the dead, lives in you. And just as God raised Christ from the dead, he will give life to your mortal bodies by this same Spirit living within you.

ROMANS 8:11 NLT

And when the Chief Shepherd appears, you will receive the crown of glory that does not fade away.

I PETER 5:4 NKJV

For we know that if our earthly house, this tent, is destroyed, we have a building from God, a house not made with hands, eternal in the heavens.

2 CORINTHIANS 5:1 NKJV

The world is passing away, and also its lusts; but the one who does the will of God lives forever.

1 JOHN 2:17 NASB

"Most assuredly, I say to you, he who hears My word and believes in Him who sent Me has everlasting life, and shall not come into judgment, but has passed from death into life."

JOHN 5:24 NKJV

That being justified by his grace, we should be made heirs according to the hope of eternal life.

TITUS 3:7 KJV

"He who loves his life loses it, and he who hates his life in this world will keep it to life eternal."

JOHN 12:25 NASB

"For this reason, they are before the throne of God; and they serve Him day and night in His temple; and He who sits on the throne will spread His tabernacle over them. They will hunger no longer, nor thirst anymore; nor will the sun beat down on them, nor any heat; for the Lamb in the center of the throne

will be their shepherd, and will guide them to springs of the
water of life; and God will wipe every tear from their eyes."

REVELATION 7:15–17 NASB

"And this is eternal life, that they may know You, the only
true God, and Jesus Christ whom You have sent."

JOHN 17:3 NKJV

We know also that the Son of God has come and has given
us understanding, so that we may know him who is true.
And we are in him who is true—even in his Son Jesus
Christ. He is the true God and eternal life.

1 JOHN 5:20 NIV

Jesus said to her, "I am the resurrection and the life; he who
believes in Me will live even if he dies, and everyone who lives
and believes in Me will never die. Do you believe this?"

JOHN 11:25–26 NASB

Blessed be the God and Father of our Lord Jesus Christ, who
according to His great mercy has caused us to be born again
to a living hope through the resurrection of Jesus Christ from
the dead, to obtain an inheritance which is imperishable and
undefiled and will not fade away, reserved in heaven for you,
who are protected by the power of God through faith for a
salvation ready to be revealed in the last time.

1 PETER 1:3–5 NASB

Keep yourselves in God's love as you wait for the mercy of our Lord Jesus Christ to bring you to eternal life.

JUDE 1:21 NIV

He will give eternal life to those who keep on doing good, seeking after the glory and honor and immortality that God offers.

ROMANS 2:7 NLT

This truth gives them the confidence that they have eternal life, which God—who does not lie—promised them before the world began.

TITUS 1:2 NLT

For God so loved the world, that he gave his only begotten Son, that whosoever believeth in him should not perish, but have everlasting life.

JOHN 3:16 KJV

And this is the testimony: that God has given us eternal life, and this life is in His Son. He who has the Son has life; he who does not have the Son of God does not have life. These things I have written to you who believe in the name of the Son of God, that you may know that you have eternal life, and that you may continue to believe in the name of the Son of God.

1 JOHN 5:11–13 NKJV

"And I give them eternal life, and they shall never perish; neither shall anyone snatch them out of My hand."

JOHN 10:28 NKJV

Let that therefore abide in you, which ye have heard from the beginning. If that which ye have heard from the beginning shall remain in you, ye also shall continue in the Son, and in the Father. And this is the promise that he hath promised us, even eternal life.

1 JOHN 2:24–25 KJV

There shall be no night there: They need no lamp nor light of the sun, for the Lord God gives them light. And they shall reign forever and ever.

REVELATION 22:5 NKJV

Behold, I tell you a mystery: We shall not all sleep, but we shall all be changed—in a moment, in the twinkling of an eye, at the last trumpet. For the trumpet will sound, and the dead will be raised incorruptible, and we shall be changed. For this corruptible must put on incorruption, and this mortal must put on immortality. So when this corruptible has put on incorruption, and this mortal has put on immortality, then shall be brought to pass the saying that is written: "Death is swallowed up in victory."

1 CORINTHIANS 15:51–54 NKJV

"Many of those who sleep in the dust of the ground will awake, these to everlasting life, but the others to disgrace and everlasting contempt."

DANIEL 12:2 NASB

Fight the good fight of faith; take hold of the eternal life to which you were called, and you made the good confession in the presence of many witnesses.

1 TIMOTHY 6:12 NASB

"In my Father's house are many rooms; if it were not so, I would have told you. I am going there to prepare a place for you. And if I go and prepare a place for you, I will come back and take you to be with me that you also may be where I am."

JOHN 14:2–3 NIV

In the future there is laid up for me the crown of righteousness, which the Lord, the righteous Judge, will award to me on that day; and not only to me, but also to all who have loved His appearing.

2 TIMOTHY 4:8 NASB

FAITH

For we walk by faith, not by sight.

2 CORINTHIANS 5:7 NKJV

In addition to all, taking up the shield of faith with which you will be able to extinguish all the flaming arrows of the evil one.

EPHESIANS 6:16 NASB

Now the purpose of the commandment is love from a pure heart, from a good conscience, and from sincere faith.

1 TIMOTHY 1:5 NKJV

Listen, my dear brothers: Has not God chosen those who are poor in the eyes of the world to be rich in faith and to inherit the kingdom he promised those who love him?

JAMES 2:5 NIV

Trust in the LORD with all your heart, and lean not on your own understanding.

PROVERBS 3:5 NKJV

"For I will certainly rescue you, and you will not fall by the sword; but you will have your own life as booty, because you have trusted in Me," declares the LORD.

JEREMIAH 39:18 NASB

Now faith is the substance of things hoped for, the evidence of things not seen.

HEBREWS 11:1 KJV

For you know that when your faith is tested, your endurance has a chance to grow. So let it grow, for when your endurance is fully developed, you will be perfect and complete, needing nothing.

JAMES 1:3–4 NLT

And He said to the woman, "Your faith has saved you; go in peace."

LUKE 7:50 NASB

This charge I commit to you, son Timothy, according to the prophecies previously made concerning you, that by them you may wage the good warfare, having faith and a good conscience.

1 TIMOTHY 1:18–19 NKJV

But as many as received Him, to them He gave the right to become children of God, even to those who believe in His name.

JOHN 1:12 NASB

And my speech and my preaching were not with persuasive words of human wisdom, but in demonstration of the Spirit and of power, that your faith should not be in the wisdom of men but in the power of God.

1 CORINTHIANS 2:4–5 NKJV

"Blessed is the man who trusts in the LORD and whose trust is the LORD. For he will be like a tree planted by the water, that extends its roots by a stream and will not fear when the heat comes; but its leaves will be green, and it will not be anxious in a year of drought nor cease to yield fruit."

JEREMIAH 17:7–8 NASB

"Have faith in God," Jesus answered. "I tell you the truth, if anyone says to this mountain, 'Go, throw yourself into the sea,' and does not doubt in his heart but believes that what he says will happen, it will be done for him. Therefore I tell you, whatever you ask for in prayer, believe that you have received it, and it will be yours."

MARK 11:22–24 NIV

That He would grant you, according to the riches of His glory, to be strengthened with might through His Spirit in the inner man, that Christ may dwell in your hearts through faith; that you, being rooted and grounded in love, may be able to comprehend with all the saints what is the width and length and depth and height—to know the love of Christ which passes knowledge; that you may be filled with all the fullness of God.

EPHESIANS 3:16–19 NKJV

Watch, stand fast in the faith.

1 CORINTHIANS 16:13 NKJV

Thou wilt keep him in perfect peace, whose mind is stayed on thee: because he trusteth in thee.

ISAIAH 26:3 KJV

It is no longer I who live, but Christ lives in me. So I live in this earthly body by trusting in the Son of God, who loved me and gave himself for me.

GALATIANS 2:20 NLT

For in it the righteousness of God is revealed from faith to faith; as it is written, "BUT THE RIGHTEOUS man SHALL LIVE BY FAITH."

ROMANS 1:17 NASB

So the Lord said, "If you have faith as a mustard seed, you can say to this mulberry tree, 'Be pulled up by the roots and be planted in the sea,' and it would obey you."

LUKE 17:6 NKJV

Let us go right into the presence of God with sincere hearts fully trusting him. For our guilty consciences have been sprinkled with Christ's blood to make us clean, and our bodies have been washed with pure water.

HEBREWS 10:22 NLT

For you are all sons of God through faith in Christ Jesus.

GALATIANS 3:26 NKJV

And though you have not seen Him, you love Him, and though you do not see Him now, but believe in Him, you greatly rejoice with joy inexpressible and full of glory.

1 PETER 1:8 NASB

"Everything is possible for him who believes."

MARK 9:23 NIV

Is any one of you sick? He should call the elders of the church to pray over him and anoint him with oil in the name of the Lord. And the prayer offered in faith will make the sick person well; the Lord will raise him up. If he has sinned, he will be forgiven.

JAMES 5:14–15 NIV

Jesus saith unto him, Thomas, because thou hast seen me, thou hast believed: blessed are they that have not seen, and yet have believed.

JOHN 20:29 KJV

But if any of you lacks wisdom, let him ask of God, who gives to all generously and without reproach, and it will be given to him. But he must ask in faith without any doubting, for the one who doubts is like the surf of the sea, driven and tossed by the wind.

JAMES 1:5–6 NASB

And without faith it is impossible to please Him, for he who comes to God must believe that He is and that He is a rewarder of those who seek Him.

Hebrews 11:6 NASB

So then faith comes by hearing, and hearing by the word of God.

Romans 10:17 NKJV

Finances

A good name is to be chosen rather than great riches, loving favor rather than silver and gold. . . . By humility and the fear of the Lord are riches and honor and life.

Proverbs 22:1, 4 NKJV

Make sure that your character is free from the love of money, being content with what you have; for He Himself has said, "I will never desert you, nor will I ever forsake you."

Hebrews 13:5 NASB

The rich ruleth over the poor, and the borrower is servant to the lender.

Proverbs 22:7 KJV

Do not withhold good from those who deserve it when it's in your power to help them. If you can help your neighbor now, don't say, "Come back tomorrow, and then I'll help you."

PROVERBS 3:27–28 NLT

"Give, and it will be given to you: good measure, pressed down, shaken together, and running over will be put into your bosom. For with the same measure that you use, it will be measured back to you."

LUKE 6:38 NKJV

But those who want to get rich fall into temptation and a snare and many foolish and harmful desires which plunge men into ruin and destruction. For the love of money is a root of all sorts of evil, and some by longing for it have wandered away from the faith and pierced themselves with many griefs. But flee from these things, you man of God, and pursue righteousness, godliness, faith, love, perseverance and gentleness.

1 TIMOTHY 6:9–11 NASB

In this case, moreover, it is required of stewards that one be found trustworthy.

1 CORINTHIANS 4:2 NASB

"For which of you, intending to build a tower, does not sit down first and count the cost, whether he has enough to finish it—lest, after he has laid the foundation, and is not able to finish, all who see it begin to mock him, saying, 'This man began to build and was not able to finish.' "

LUKE 14:28–30 NKJV

Do not be among those who give pledges, among those who become guarantors for debts. If you have nothing with which to pay, why should he take your bed from under you?

PROVERBS 22:26–27 NASB

And He said to them, "Render therefore to Caesar the things that are Caesar's, and to God the things that are God's."

MATTHEW 22:21 NKJV

Lord, who shall abide in thy tabernacle? who shall dwell in thy holy hill? . . . He that putteth not out his money to usury, nor taketh reward against the innocent. He that doeth these things shall never be moved.

PSALM 15:1, 5 KJV

And it is a good thing to receive wealth from God and the good health to enjoy it. To enjoy your work and accept your lot in life—this is indeed a gift from God.

ECCLESIASTES 5:19 NLT

"Every man shall give as he is able, according to the blessing of the LORD your God which He has given you."

DEUTERONOMY 16:17 NASB

Riches do not profit in the day of wrath, but righteousness delivers from death.

PROVERBS 11:4 NKJV

He who trusts in his riches will fall, but the righteous will flourish like the green leaf.

PROVERBS 11:28 NASB

"I tell you, use worldly wealth to gain friends for yourselves, so that when it is gone, you will be welcomed into eternal dwellings. Whoever can be trusted with very little can also be trusted with much, and whoever is dishonest with very little will also be dishonest with much. So if you have not been trustworthy in handling worldly wealth, who will trust you with true riches? And if you have not been trustworthy with someone else's property, who will give you property of your own?"

LUKE 16:9–12 NIV

Some who are poor pretend to be rich; others who are rich pretend to be poor.

PROVERBS 13:7 NLT

"No one can serve two masters; for either he will hate the one and love the other, or else he will be loyal to the one and despise the other. You cannot serve God and mammon."

MATTHEW 6:24 NKJV

"I have shown you in every way, by laboring like this, that you must support the weak. And remember the words of the Lord Jesus, that He said, 'It is more blessed to give than to receive.' "

ACTS 20:35 NKJV

"But you shall remember the LORD your God, for it is He who is giving you power to make wealth, that He may confirm His covenant which He swore to your fathers, as it is this day."

DEUTERONOMY 8:18 NASB

"So when you give to the needy, do not announce it with trumpets, as the hypocrites do in the synagogues and on the streets, to be honored by men. I tell you the truth, they have received their reward in full. But when you give to the needy, do not let your left hand know what your right hand is doing, so that your giving may be in secret. Then your Father, who sees what is done in secret, will reward you."

MATTHEW 6:2–4 NIV

There is a grievous evil which I have seen under the sun: riches being hoarded by their owner to his hurt. When those riches were lost through a bad investment and he had fathered a son, then there was nothing to support him. As he had come naked from his mother's womb, so will he return as he came. He will take nothing from the fruit of his labor that he can carry in his hand.

ECCLESIASTES 5:13–15 NASB

Command those who are rich in this present age not to be haughty, nor to trust in uncertain riches but in the living God, who gives us richly all things to enjoy.

1 TIMOTHY 6:17 NKJV

Honour the LORD with thy substance, and with the firstfruits of all thine increase: So shall thy barns be filled with plenty, and thy presses shall burst out with new wine.

PROVERBS 3:9–10 KJV

And He said to them, "Take heed and beware of covetousness, for one's life does not consist in the abundance of the things he possesses."

LUKE 12:15 NKJV

One who is gracious to a poor man lends to the LORD, and He will repay him for his good deed.

PROVERBS 19:17 NASB

Each man should give what he has decided in his heart to give, not reluctantly or under compulsion, for God loves a cheerful giver.

2 CORINTHIANS 9:7 NIV

Let the lowly brother glory in his exaltation, but the rich in his humiliation, because as a flower of the field he will pass away. For no sooner has the sun risen with a burning heat than it withers the grass; its flower falls, and its beautiful appearance perishes. So the rich man also will fade away in his pursuits.

JAMES 1:9–11 NKJV

"And others are the ones on whom seed was sown among the thorns; these are the ones who have heard the word, but the worries of the world, and the deceitfulness of riches, and the desires for other things enter in and choke the word, and it becomes unfruitful."

MARK 4:18–19 NASB

Lay not up for yourselves treasures upon earth, where moth and rust doth corrupt, and where thieves break through and steal: But lay up for yourselves treasures in heaven, where neither moth nor rust doth corrupt, and where thieves do not break through nor steal: For where your treasure is, there will your heart be also.

MATTHEW 6:19–21 KJV

After all, we brought nothing with us when we came into the world, and we can't take anything with us when we leave it. So if we have enough food and clothing, let us be content.

1 TIMOTHY 6:7–8 NLT

If then you were raised with Christ, seek those things which are above, where Christ is, sitting at the right hand of God. Set your mind on things above, not on things on the earth.

COLOSSIANS 3:1–2 NKJV

Do not trust in oppression and do not vainly hope in robbery; if riches increase, do not set your heart upon them.

PSALM 62:10 NASB

"Give generously to the poor, not grudgingly, for the LORD your God will bless you in everything you do."

DEUTERONOMY 15:10 NLT

Wealth obtained by fraud dwindles, but the one who gathers by labor increases it.

PROVERBS 13:11 NASB

"Therefore I say to you, do not worry about your life, what you will eat or what you will drink; nor about your body, what you will put on. Is not life more than food and the body more than clothing? Look at the birds of the air, for they neither sow nor reap nor gather into barns; yet your heavenly Father feeds them. Are you not of more value than they? Which of you by worrying can add one cubit to his stature? So why do you worry about clothing? Consider the lilies of the field, how they grow: they neither toil nor spin; and yet I say to you that even Solomon in all his glory was not arrayed like one of these. Now if God so clothes the grass of the field, which today is, and tomorrow is thrown into the oven, will He not much more clothe you, O you of little faith? Therefore do not worry, saying, 'What shall we eat?' or 'What shall we drink?' or 'What shall we wear?' For after all these things the Gentiles seek. For your heavenly Father knows that you need all these things. But seek first the kingdom of God and His righteousness, and all these things shall be added to you."

MATTHEW 6:25–33 NKJV

FORGIVENESS

Take heed to yourselves: If thy brother trespass against thee, rebuke him; and if he repent, forgive him. And if he trespass against thee seven times in a day, and seven times in a day turn again to thee, saying, I repent; thou shalt forgive him.

LUKE 17:3–4 KJV

"Do not judge, and you will not be judged. Do not condemn, and you will not be condemned. Forgive, and you will be forgiven."

LUKE 6:37 NIV

"No more shall every man teach his neighbor, and every man his brother, saying, 'Know the LORD,' for they all shall know Me, from the least of them to the greatest of them, says the LORD. For I will forgive their iniquity, and their sin I will remember no more."

JEREMIAH 31:34 NKJV

The discretion of a man makes him slow to anger, and his glory is to overlook a transgression.

PROVERBS 19:11 NKJV

"But I say to you, do not resist an evil person; but whoever slaps you on your right cheek, turn the other to him also. If anyone wants to sue you and take your shirt, let him have your coat also. Whoever forces you to go one mile, go with him two."

MATTHEW 5:39–41 NASB

"And forgive us our sins, for we also forgive everyone who is indebted to us."

LUKE 11:4 NKJV

Who is a God like You, pardoning iniquity and passing over the transgression of the remnant of His heritage? He does not retain His anger forever, because He delights in mercy.

MICAH 7:18 NKJV

If we confess our sins, He is faithful and righteous to forgive us our sins and to cleanse us from all unrighteousness.

1 JOHN 1:9 NASB

Bless the LORD, O my soul, and forget none of His benefits; who pardons all your iniquities, who heals all your diseases.

PSALM 103:2–3 NASB

And be ye kind one to another, tenderhearted, forgiving one another, even as God for Christ's sake hath forgiven you.

EPHESIANS 4:32 KJV

"None of their past sins will be brought up again, for they have done what is just and right, and they will surely live."

EZEKIEL 33:16 NLT

Be gracious to me, O God, according to Your lovingkindness; according to the greatness of Your compassion blot out my transgressions.

PSALM 51:1 NASB

"But when you are praying, first forgive anyone you are holding a grudge against, so that your Father in heaven will forgive your sins, too."

MARK 11:25 NLT

"For this is My blood of the new covenant, which is shed for many for the remission of sins."

MATTHEW 26:28 NKJV

Not returning evil for evil or insult for insult, but giving a blessing instead; for you were called for the very purpose that you might inherit a blessing.

1 PETER 3:9 NASB

How blessed is he whose transgression is forgiven, whose sin is covered!

PSALM 32:1 NASB

Then Peter came to Jesus and asked, "Lord, how many times shall I forgive my brother when he sins against me? Up to seven times?" Jesus answered, "I tell you, not seven times, but seventy-seven times."

MATTHEW 18:21–22 NIV

"For I will forgive their wickedness and will remember their sins no more."

HEBREWS 8:12 NIV

Therefore, as the elect of God, holy and beloved, put on tender mercies, kindness, humility, meekness, long-suffering; bearing with one another, and forgiving one another, if anyone has a complaint against another; even as Christ forgave you, so you also must do.

COLOSSIANS 3:12–13 NKJV

"For if you forgive men their trespasses, your heavenly Father will also forgive you. But if you do not forgive men their trespasses, neither will your Father forgive your trespasses."

MATTHEW 6:14–15 NKJV

GENEROSITY

They share freely and give generously to those in need. Their good deeds will be remembered forever. They will have influence and honor.

PSALM 112:9 NLT

And He saw a poor widow putting in two small copper coins. And He said, "Truly I say to you, this poor widow put in more than all of them; for they all out of their surplus put into the offering; but she out of her poverty put in all that she had to live on."

LUKE 21:2–4 NASB

"But when you give a reception, invite the poor, the crippled, the lame, the blind, and you will be blessed, since they do not have the means to repay you; for you will be repaid at the resurrection of the righteous."

LUKE 14:13–14 NASB

Command those who are rich in this present world not to be arrogant nor to put their hope in wealth, which is so uncertain, but to put their hope in God, who richly provides us with everything for our enjoyment. Command them to do good, to be rich in good deeds, and to be generous and willing to share.

1 TIMOTHY 6:17–18 NIV

He answereth and saith unto them, He that hath two coats, let him impart to him that hath none; and he that hath meat, let him do likewise.

LUKE 3:11 KJV

He who despises his neighbor sins, but blessed is he who is kind to the needy.

PROVERBS 14:21 NIV

"If one of your brethren becomes poor, and falls into poverty among you, then you shall help him, like a stranger or a sojourner, that he may live with you."

LEVITICUS 25:35 NKJV

Do not withhold good from those who deserve it, when it is in your power to act. Do not say to your neighbor, "Come back later; I'll give it tomorrow"—when you now have it with you.

PROVERBS 3:27–28 NIV

"When you give to someone in need, don't do as the hypocrites do—blowing trumpets in the synagogues and streets to call attention to their acts of charity! I tell you the truth, they have received all the reward they will ever get. But when you give to someone in need, don't let your left hand know what your right hand is doing. Give your gifts in private, and your Father, who sees everything, will reward you."

MATTHEW 6:2–4 NLT

If a woman who is a believer has relatives who are widows, she must take care of them and not put the responsibility on the church. Then the church can care for the widows who are truly alone.

1 TIMOTHY 5:16 NLT

If a brother or sister be naked, and destitute of daily food, and one of you say unto them, Depart in peace, be ye warmed and filled; notwithstanding ye give them not those things which are needful to the body; what doth it profit?

JAMES 2:15–16 KJV

There will always be poor people in the land. Therefore I command you to be openhanded toward your brothers and toward the poor and needy in your land.

Deuteronomy 15:11 niv

Oh, the joys of those who are kind to the poor! The Lord rescues them when they are in trouble. The Lord protects them and keeps them alive. He gives them prosperity in the land and rescues them from their enemies.

Psalm 41:1–2 nlt

Each man should give what he has decided in his heart to give, not reluctantly or under compulsion, for God loves a cheerful giver.

2 Corinthians 9:7 niv

"Give, and you will receive. Your gift will return to you in full—pressed down, shaken together to make room for more, running over, and poured into your lap. The amount you give will determine the amount you get back."

Luke 6:38 nlt

I tell you the truth, anyone who gives you a cup of water in my name because you belong to Christ will certainly not lose his reward.

Mark 9:41 niv

Every man shall give as he is able, according to the blessing of the LORD thy God which he hath given thee.

DEUTERONOMY 16:17 KJV

For you know the grace of our Lord Jesus Christ, that though He was rich, yet for your sake He became poor, so that you through His poverty might become rich.

2 CORINTHIANS 8:9 NASB

He who is kind to the poor lends to the LORD, and he will reward him for what he has done.

PROVERBS 19:17 NIV

Is it not to share your bread with the hungry, and that you bring to your house the poor who are cast out; when you see the naked, that you cover him, and not hide yourself from your own flesh? Then your light shall break forth like the morning, your healing shall spring forth speedily, and your righteousness shall go before you; the glory of the LORD shall be your rear guard.

ISAIAH 58:7–8 NKJV

I have shewed you all things, how that so labouring ye ought to support the weak, and to remember the words of the Lord Jesus, how he said, It is more blessed to give than to receive.

ACTS 20:35 KJV

GENTLENESS

"Take my yoke upon you and learn from me, for I am gentle and humble in heart, and you will find rest for your souls."

MATTHEW 11:29 NIV

The lowly will possess the land and will live in peace and prosperity.

PSALM 37:11 NLT

Now I, Paul, myself am pleading with you by the meekness and gentleness of Christ—who in presence am lowly among you, but being absent am bold toward you.

2 CORINTHIANS 10:1 NKJV

Remind the people to be subject to rulers and authorities, to be obedient, to be ready to do whatever is good, to slander no one, to be peaceable and considerate, and to show true humility toward all men.

TITUS 3:1–2 NIV

Like a shepherd He will tend His flock, in His arm He will gather the lambs and carry them in His bosom; He will gently lead the nursing ewes.

ISAIAH 40:11 NASB

The meek will he guide in judgment: and the meek will he teach his way.

PSALM 25:9 KJV

But the Holy Spirit produces this kind of fruit in our lives: love, joy, peace, patience, kindness, goodness, faithfulness.

GALATIANS 5:22 NLT

And the servant of the Lord must not strive; but be gentle unto all men, apt to teach, patient, in meekness instructing those that oppose themselves; if God peradventure will give them repentance to the acknowledging of the truth; and that they may recover themselves out of the snare of the devil, who are taken captive by him at his will.

2 TIMOTHY 2:24–26 KJV

The poor shall eat and be satisfied; those who seek Him will praise the LORD. Let your heart live forever!

PSALM 22:26 NKJV

The LORD supports the afflicted; He brings down the wicked to the ground.

PSALM 147:6 NASB

For the LORD takes delight in his people; he crowns the humble with salvation.

PSALM 149:4 NIV

But the wisdom that is from above is first pure, then peaceable, gentle, and easy to be intreated, full of mercy and good fruits, without partiality, and without hypocrisy.

JAMES 3:17 KJV

Thou hast also given me the shield of thy salvation: and thy gentleness hath made me great.

2 SAMUEL 22:36 KJV

As apostles of Christ we certainly had a right to make some demands of you, but instead we were like children among you. Or we were like a mother feeding and caring for her own children.

1 THESSALONIANS 2:7 NLT

GOD'S LOVE

"For God loved the world so much that he gave his one and only Son, so that everyone who believes in him will not perish but have eternal life."

JOHN 3:16 NLT

"Are not five sparrows sold for two copper coins? And not one of them is forgotten before God. But the very hairs of your head are all numbered. Do not fear therefore; you are of more value than many sparrows."

LUKE 12:6–7 NKJV

For it is You who blesses the righteous man, O LORD, You surround him with favor as with a shield.

PSALM 5:12 NASB

And we know that God causes all things to work together for good to those who love God, to those who are called according to His purpose.

ROMANS 8:28 NASB

Those who know your name trust in you, for you, O LORD, do not abandon those who search for you.

PSALM 9:10 NLT

"Lo, I am with you always, even to the end of the age."

MATTHEW 28:20 NASB

Now hope does not disappoint, because the love of God has been poured out in our hearts by the Holy Spirit who was given to us.

ROMANS 5:5 NKJV

But the LORD is with me as a mighty, awesome One. Therefore my persecutors will stumble, and will not prevail. They will be greatly ashamed, for they will not prosper. Their everlasting confusion will never be forgotten.

JEREMIAH 20:11 NKJV

"I knew that you are a gracious and compassionate God, slow to anger and abounding in love, a God who relents from sending calamity."

JONAH 4:2 NIV

"For the LORD your God is a compassionate God; He will not fail you nor destroy you nor forget the covenant with your fathers which He swore to them."

DEUTERONOMY 4:31 NASB

He will fulfil the desire of them that fear him: he also will hear their cry, and will save them. The LORD preserveth all them that love him: but all the wicked will he destroy.

PSALM 145:19–20 KJV

"I will heal their backsliding, I will love them freely, for My anger has turned away from him."

HOSEA 14:4 NKJV

But You, O Lord, are a God merciful and gracious, slow to anger and abundant in lovingkindness and truth.

PSALM 86:15 NASB

The LORD will guard your going out and your coming in from this time forth and forever.

PSALM 121:8 NASB

God showed how much he loved us by sending his one and only Son into the world so that we might have eternal life through him. This is real love—not that we loved God, but that he loved us and sent his Son as a sacrifice to take away our sins.

1 JOHN 4:9–10 NLT

And we have known and believed the love that God has for us. God is love, and he who abides in love abides in God, and God in him.

1 JOHN 4:16 NKJV

For I am persuaded that neither death nor life, nor angels nor principalities nor powers, nor things present nor things to come, nor height nor depth, nor any other created thing, shall be able to separate us from the love of God which is in Christ Jesus our Lord.

ROMANS 8:38–39 NKJV

As for God, His way is blameless; the word of the LORD is tried; He is a shield to all who take refuge in Him.

PSALM 18:30 NASB

For the Father himself loveth you, because ye have loved me, and have believed that I came out from God.

JOHN 16:27 KJV

Every good gift and every perfect gift is from above, and comes down from the Father of lights, with whom there is no variation or shadow of turning. Of His own will He brought us forth by the word of truth, that we might be a kind of firstfruits of His creatures.

JAMES 1:17–18 NKJV

And my God will meet all your needs according to his glorious riches in Christ Jesus.

PHILIPPIANS 4:19 NIV

Many are the sorrows of the wicked, but he who trusts in the LORD, lovingkindness shall surround him.

PSALM 32:10 NASB

But God showed his great love for us by sending Christ to die for us while we were still sinners.

ROMANS 5:8 NLT

Behold what manner of love the Father has bestowed on us, that we should be called children of God!

1 JOHN 3:1 NKJV

GOD'S PROVISION

Therefore I say unto you, Take no thought for your life, what ye shall eat, or what ye shall drink; nor yet for your body, what ye shall put on. Is not the life more than meat, and the body than raiment? Behold the fowls of the air: for they sow not, neither do they reap, nor gather into barns; yet your heavenly Father feedeth them. Are ye not much better than they? Which of you by taking thought can add one cubit unto his stature? And why take ye thought for raiment? Consider the lilies of the field, how they grow; they toil not, neither do they spin: And yet I say unto you, That even Solomon in all his glory was not arrayed like one of these. Wherefore, if God so clothe the grass of the field, which to day is, and to morrow is cast into the oven, shall he not much more clothe you, O ye of little faith? Therefore take no thought, saying, What shall we eat? or, What shall we drink? or, Wherewithal shall we be clothed? (For after all these things do the Gentiles seek:) for your heavenly Father knoweth that ye have need of all these things. But seek ye first the kingdom of God, and his righteousness; and all these things shall be added unto you.

MATTHEW 6:25–33 KJV

But my God shall supply all your need according to his riches in glory by Christ Jesus.

PHILIPPIANS 4:19 KJV

Command those who are rich in this present world not to be arrogant nor to put their hope in wealth, which is so uncertain, but to put their hope in God, who richly provides us with everything for our enjoyment.

1 TIMOTHY 6:17 NIV

The young lions do lack and suffer hunger; but they who seek the LORD shall not be in want of any good thing.

PSALM 34:10 NASB

He has given food to those who fear Him; He will ever be mindful of His covenant.

PSALM 111:5 NKJV

GRATITUDE

O give thanks to the LORD, for He is good; for His loving-kindness is everlasting.

1 CHRONICLES 16:34 NASB

For every creature of God is good, and nothing to be refused, if it be received with thanksgiving.

1 TIMOTHY 4:4 KJV

But thanks be to God, which giveth us the victory through our Lord Jesus Christ.

1 CORINTHIANS 15:57 KJV

Singing psalms and hymns and spiritual songs among yourselves, and making music to the Lord in your hearts. And give thanks for everything to God the Father in the name of our Lord Jesus Christ.

EPHESIANS 5:19–20 NLT

Is anyone among you suffering? Then he must pray. Is anyone cheerful? He is to sing praises.

JAMES 5:13 NASB

Oh come, let us sing to the LORD! Let us shout joyfully to the Rock of our salvation. Let us come before His presence with thanksgiving; let us shout joyfully to Him with psalms.

PSALM 95:1–2 NKJV

In everything give thanks; for this is God's will for you in Christ Jesus.

1 THESSALONIANS 5:18 NASB

I will wash my hands in innocence; so I will go about Your altar, O LORD, that I may proclaim with the voice of thanksgiving, and tell of all Your wondrous works.

PSALM 26:6–7 NKJV

I will praise You, O LORD, with my whole heart; I will tell of all Your marvelous works.

PSALM 9:1 NKJV

I will praise the name of God with a song, and will magnify Him with thanksgiving. This also shall please the LORD better than an ox or bull, which has horns and hooves.

PSALM 69:30–31 NKJV

He took the seven loaves and the fish; and giving thanks, He broke them and started giving them to the disciples, and the disciples gave them to the people.

MATTHEW 15:36 NASB

And whatever you do or say, do it as a representative of the Lord Jesus, giving thanks through him to God the Father.

COLOSSIANS 3:17 NLT

It is good to give thanks to the LORD, and to sing praises to Your name, O Most High; to declare Your lovingkindness in the morning, and Your faithfulness every night.

PSALM 92:1–2 NKJV

Therefore, since we are receiving a kingdom that cannot be shaken, let us be thankful, and so worship God acceptably with reverence and awe.

HEBREWS 12:28 NIV

Oh, give thanks to the LORD, for He is good! For His mercy endures forever.

PSALM 136:1 NKJV

And in that day you will say, "Give thanks to the LORD, call on His name. Make known His deeds among the peoples; make them remember that His name is exalted."

ISAIAH 12:4 NASB

HONESTY

Lying lips are an abomination to the LORD, but those who deal faithfully are His delight.

PROVERBS 12:22 NASB

"I will maintain my righteousness and never let go of it; my conscience will not reproach me as long as I live."

JOB 27:6 NIV

Honest weights and scales are the LORD's; all the weights in the bag are His work.

PROVERBS 16:11 NKJV

Pray for us, for we are sure that we have a good conscience, desiring to conduct ourselves honorably in all things.

HEBREWS 13:18 NASB

"In everything, therefore, treat people the same way you want them to treat you, for this is the Law and the Prophets."

MATTHEW 7:12 NASB

But we have renounced the hidden things of shame, not walking in craftiness nor handling the word of God deceitfully, but by manifestation of the truth commending ourselves to every man's conscience in the sight of God.

2 CORINTHIANS 4:2 NKJV

The LORD abhors dishonest scales, but accurate weights are his delight.

PROVERBS 11:1 NIV

"Do not use dishonest standards when measuring length, weight, or volume. Your scales and weights must be accurate. Your containers for measuring dry goods or liquids must be accurate."

LEVITICUS 19:35–36 NLT

"Do not steal. Do not deceive or cheat one another."

LEVITICUS 19:11 NLT

Providing honorable things, not only in the sight of the Lord, but also in the sight of men.

2 CORINTHIANS 8:21 NKJV

And herein do I exercise myself, to have always a conscience void of offence toward God, and toward men.

ACTS 24:16 KJV

Finally, brethren, whatever is true, whatever is honorable, whatever is right, whatever is pure, whatever is lovely, whatever is of good repute, if there is any excellence and if anything worthy of praise, dwell on these things. The things you have learned and received and heard and seen in me, practice these things, and the God of peace will be with you.

PHILIPPIANS 4:8–9 NASB

Who may ascend into the hill of the LORD? And who may stand in His holy place? He who has clean hands and a pure heart, who has not lifted up his soul to falsehood and has not sworn deceitfully.

PSALM 24:3–4 NASB

Do not lie to one another, since you have put off the old man with his deeds, and have put on the new man who is renewed in knowledge according to the image of Him who created him.

COLOSSIANS 3:9–10 NKJV

HUMILITY

By humility and the fear of the LORD are riches and honor and life.

PROVERBS 22:4 NKJV

But he giveth more grace. Wherefore he saith, God resisteth the proud, but giveth grace unto the humble. Submit yourselves therefore to God. Resist the devil, and he will flee from you.

JAMES 4:6–7 KJV

The humble have seen it and are glad; you who seek God, let your heart revive.

PSALM 69:32 NASB

When pride cometh, then cometh shame: but with the lowly is wisdom.

PROVERBS 11:2 KJV

"I tell you, this sinner, not the Pharisee, returned home justified before God. For those who exalt themselves will be humbled, and those who humble themselves will be exalted."

LUKE 18:14 NLT

For thus says the High and Lofty One who inhabits eternity, whose name is Holy: "I dwell in the high and holy place, with him who has a contrite and humble spirit, to revive the spirit of the humble, and to revive the heart of the contrite ones."

ISAIAH 57:15 NKJV

The fear of the LORD is the instruction for wisdom, and before honor comes humility.

PROVERBS 15:33 NASB

And whosoever shall exalt himself shall be abased; and he that shall humble himself shall be exalted.

MATTHEW 23:12 KJV

You younger men, likewise, be subject to your elders; and all of you, clothe yourselves with humility toward one another, for GOD IS OPPOSED TO THE PROUD, BUT GIVES GRACE TO THE HUMBLE. Therefore humble yourselves under the mighty hand of God, that He may exalt you at the proper time.

1 PETER 5:5–6 NASB

"Truly, truly, I say to you, that you will weep and lament, but the world will rejoice; you will grieve, but your grief will be turned into joy."

JOHN 16:20 NASB

For though the LORD is exalted, yet He regards the lowly, but the haughty He knows from afar.

PSALM 138:6 NASB

He mocks proud mockers but gives grace to the humble.

PROVERBS 3:34 NIV

Therefore if there is any consolation in Christ, if any comfort of love, if any fellowship of the Spirit, if any affection and mercy, fulfill my joy by being like-minded, having the same love, being of one accord, of one mind. Let nothing be done through selfish ambition or conceit, but in lowliness of mind let each esteem others better than himself.

PHILIPPIANS 2:1–3 NKJV

"Therefore whoever humbles himself as this little child is the greatest in the kingdom of heaven."

MATTHEW 18:4 NKJV

Humble yourselves in the presence of the Lord, and He will exalt you.

JAMES 4:10 NASB

JOY

Dear brothers and sisters, when troubles come your way, consider it an opportunity for great joy.

JAMES 1:2 NLT

Now may the God of hope fill you with all joy and peace in believing, that you may abound in hope by the power of the Holy Spirit.

ROMANS 15:13 NKJV

Speaking to yourselves in psalms and hymns and spiritual songs, singing and making melody in your heart to the Lord.

EPHESIANS 5:19 KJV

The LORD is my strength and my shield; my heart trusted in Him, and I am helped; therefore my heart greatly rejoices, and with my song I will praise Him.

PSALM 28:7 NKJV

My lips shall greatly rejoice when I sing to You, and my soul, which You have redeemed.

PSALM 71:23 NKJV

"You will go out in joy and be led forth in peace; the mountains and hills will burst into song before you, and all the trees of the field will clap their hands."

ISAIAH 55:12 NIV

Rejoicing in hope, persevering in tribulation, devoted to prayer. . .

ROMANS 12:12 NASB

"YOU HAVE MADE KNOWN TO ME THE WAYS OF LIFE; YOU WILL MAKE ME FULL OF GLADNESS WITH YOUR PRESENCE."

ACTS 2:28 NASB

Those who plant in tears will harvest with shouts of joy. They weep as they go to plant their seed, but they sing as they return with the harvest.

PSALM 126:5–6 NLT

"These things I have spoken to you, that My joy may remain in you, and that your joy may be full."

JOHN 15:11 NKJV

"Then shall the virgin rejoice in the dance, and the young men and the old, together; for I will turn their mourning to joy, will comfort them, and make them rejoice rather than sorrow."

JEREMIAH 31:13 NKJV

But let all those that put their trust in thee rejoice: let them ever shout for joy, because thou defendest them: let them also that love thy name be joyful in thee.

PSALM 5:11 KJV

I will rejoice greatly in the LORD, my soul will exult in my God; for He has clothed me with garments of salvation, He has wrapped me with a robe of righteousness, as a bridegroom decks himself with a garland, and as a bride adorns herself with her jewels.

ISAIAH 61:10 NASB

"Until now you have asked for nothing in My name; ask and you will receive, so that your joy may be made full."

JOHN 16:24 NASB

You will show me the way of life, granting me the joy of your presence and the pleasures of living with you forever.

PSALM 16:11 NLT

"Rejoice in that day and leap for joy! For indeed your reward is great in heaven, for in like manner their fathers did to the prophets."

LUKE 6:23 NKJV

Rejoice in the Lord always. Again I will say, rejoice!

PHILIPPIANS 4:4 NKJV

"But now I come to You; and these things I speak in the world so that they may have My joy made full in themselves."

JOHN 17:13 NASB

"He will yet fill your mouth with laughter and your lips with shouting."

JOB 8:21 NASB

Rejoice in the LORD and be glad, you righteous; sing, all you who are upright in heart!

PSALM 32:11 NIV

So the ransomed of the LORD shall return, and come to Zion with singing, with everlasting joy on their heads. They shall obtain joy and gladness; sorrow and sighing shall flee away.

ISAIAH 51:11 NKJV

Rejoice evermore. . . . In every thing give thanks: for this is the will of God in Christ Jesus concerning you.

1 THESSALONIANS 5:16, 18 KJV

Shout joyfully to the LORD, all the earth. Serve the LORD with gladness; come before Him with joyful singing.

PSALM 100:1–2 NASB

A cheerful heart is good medicine, but a crushed spirit dries up the bones.

PROVERBS 17:22 NIV

JUSTICE

"Do not judge according to appearance, but judge with righteous judgment."

JOHN 7:24 NASB

He will judge the world with justice and rule the nations with fairness.

PSALM 9:8 NLT

"You shall do no injustice in judgment. You shall not be partial to the poor, nor honor the person of the mighty. In righteousness you shall judge your neighbor."

LEVITICUS 19:15 NKJV

"You shall not pervert justice; you shall not show partiality, nor take a bribe, for a bribe blinds the eyes of the wise and twists the words of the righteous. You shall follow what is altogether just, that you may live and inherit the land which the LORD your God is giving you."

DEUTERONOMY 16:19–20 NKJV

. . .[Jesus] whom God displayed publicly as a propitiation in His blood through faith. This was to demonstrate His righteousness, because in the forbearance of God He passed over the sins previously committed.

ROMANS 3:25 NASB

He will bring forth your righteousness as the light and your judgment as the noonday.

PSALM 37:6 NASB

Thus speaketh the LORD of hosts, saying, Execute true judgment, and shew mercy and compassions every man to his brother.

ZECHARIAH 7:9 KJV

And that no man transgress and defraud his brother in the matter because the Lord is the avenger in all these things, just as we also told you before and solemnly warned you. For God has not called us for the purpose of impurity, but in sanctification. So, he who rejects this is not rejecting man but the God who gives His Holy Spirit to you.

1 THESSALONIANS 4:6–8 NASB

Thus says the LORD: "Execute judgment and righteousness, and deliver the plundered out of the hand of the oppressor. Do no wrong and do no violence to the stranger, the fatherless, or the widow, nor shed innocent blood in this place."

JEREMIAH 22:3 NKJV

Hate evil, love good, and establish justice in the gate!

AMOS 5:15 NASB

He loveth righteousness and judgment: the earth is full of the goodness of the LORD.

PSALM 33:5 KJV

"Learn to do good; seek justice, reprove the ruthless, defend the orphan, plead for the widow."

ISAIAH 1:17 NASB

"A bruised reed He will not break, and smoking flax He will not quench, till He sends forth justice to victory."

MATTHEW 12:20 NKJV

Justice is a joy to the godly, but it terrifies evildoers.

PROVERBS 21:15 NLT

Blessed are those who keep justice, and he who does righteousness at all times!

PSALM 106:3 NKJV

The godly care about the rights of the poor; the wicked don't care at all.

PROVERBS 29:7 NLT

"Does our law condemn anyone without first hearing him to find out what he is doing?"

JOHN 7:51 NIV

"I will betroth you to Me forever; yes, I will betroth you to Me in righteousness and justice, in lovingkindness and mercy."

HOSEA 2:19 NKJV

For the LORD is a God of justice. Blessed are all who wait for him!

ISAIAH 30:18 NIV

"O Jacob My servant, do not fear," declares the LORD, "for I am with you. For I will make a full end of all the nations where I have driven you, yet I will not make a full end of you; but I will correct you properly and by no means leave you unpunished."

JEREMIAH 46:28 NASB

It is well with the man who is gracious and lends; he will maintain his cause in judgment.

PSALM 112:5 NASB

Moreover I saw under the sun: In the place of judgment, wickedness was there; and in the place of righteousness, iniquity was there. I said in my heart, "God shall judge the righteous and the wicked, for there is a time there for every purpose and for every work."

ECCLESIASTES 3:16–17 NKJV

"If there is a dispute between men. . .they come to court, that the judges may judge them, and they justify the righteous and condemn the wicked."

DEUTERONOMY 25:1 NKJV

But if ye had known what this meaneth, I will have mercy, and not sacrifice, ye would not have condemned the guiltless.

MATTHEW 12:7 KJV

Thus says the LORD, "Preserve justice and do righteousness, for My salvation is about to come and My righteousness to be revealed."

ISAIAH 56:1 NASB

Therefore, my beloved brethren, be steadfast, immovable, always abounding in the work of the Lord, knowing that your labor is not in vain in the Lord.

1 CORINTHIANS 15:58 NKJV

"You shall not circulate a false report. Do not put your hand with the wicked to be an unrighteous witness. You shall not follow a crowd to do evil; nor shall you testify in a dispute so as to turn aside after many to pervert justice. You shall not show partiality to a poor man in his dispute."

EXODUS 23:1–3 NKJV

LABOR

For the LORD your God will bless you in all your harvest and in all the work of your hands, and your joy will be complete.

DEUTERONOMY 16:15 NIV

When you shall eat of the fruit of your hands, you will be happy and it will be well with you.

PSALM 128:2 NASB

"But you, be strong and do not let your hands be weak, for your work shall be rewarded!"

2 CHRONICLES 15:7 NKJV

Do not love sleep, lest you come to poverty; open your eyes, and you will be satisfied with bread.

PROVERBS 20:13 NKJV

For even when we were with you, we used to give you this order: if anyone is not willing to work, then he is not to eat, either.

2 THESSALONIANS 3:10 NASB

Whatsoever thy hand findeth to do, do it with thy might; for there is no work, nor device, nor knowledge, nor wisdom, in the grave, whither thou goest.

ECCLESIASTES 9:10 KJV

Let the favor of the Lord our God be upon us; and confirm for us the work of our hands; yes, confirm the work of our hands.

PSALM 90:17 NASB

He who has been stealing must steal no longer, but must work, doing something useful with his own hands, that he may have something to share with those in need.

EPHESIANS 4:28 NIV

"For the Lord your God has blessed you in all that you have done; He has known your wanderings through this great wilderness. These forty years the Lord your God has been with you; you have not lacked a thing."

Deuteronomy 2:7 nasb

He becometh poor that dealeth with a slack hand: but the hand of the diligent maketh rich.

Proverbs 10:4 kjv

A hard worker has plenty of food, but a person who chases fantasies has no sense.

Proverbs 12:11 nlt

Now he who plants and he who waters are one, and each one will receive his own reward according to his own labor.

1 Corinthians 3:8 nkjv

Then I heard a voice from heaven saying to me, "Write: 'Blessed are the dead who die in the Lord from now on.' " "Yes," says the Spirit, "that they may rest from their labors, and their works follow them."

Revelation 14:13 nkjv

Do you see a man skilled in his work? He will stand before kings; He will not stand before obscure men.

Proverbs 22:29 nasb

Make it your ambition to lead a quiet life and attend to your own business and work with your hands, just as we commanded you, so that you will behave properly toward outsiders and not be in any need.

1 Thessalonians 4:11–12 NASB

"Six days you shall labor and do all your work, but the seventh day is the Sabbath of the Lord your God. In it you shall do no work: you, nor your son, nor your daughter, nor your male servant, nor your female servant, nor your cattle, nor your stranger who is within your gates."

Exodus 20:9–10 NKJV

Loving God

"But from there you will seek the Lord your God, and you will find Him if you seek Him with all your heart and with all your soul."

Deuteronomy 4:29 NKJV

But if anyone loves God, he is known by Him.

1 Corinthians 8:3 NASB

The Lord watches over all who love him, but all the wicked he will destroy.

Psalm 145:20 NIV

"So be very careful to love the LORD your God."

JOSHUA 23:11 NLT

Do not love the world or the things in the world. If anyone loves the world, the love of the Father is not in him.

1 JOHN 2:15 NKJV

And we know that God causes all things to work together for good to those who love God, to those who are called according to His purpose.

ROMANS 8:28 NASB

Jesus said unto them, If God were your Father, ye would love me: for I proceeded forth and came from God; neither came I of myself, but he sent me.

JOHN 8:42 KJV

Therefore be imitators of God as dear children. And walk in love, as Christ also has loved us and given Himself for us, an offering and a sacrifice to God for a sweet-smelling aroma.

EPHESIANS 5:1–2 NKJV

"And you shall love the LORD your God with all your heart, with all your soul, with all your mind, and with all your strength. This is the first commandment."

MARK 12:30 NKJV

For God is not unjust so as to forget your work and the love which you have shown toward His name, in having ministered and in still ministering to the saints.

HEBREWS 6:10 NASB

"I love those who love me; and those who diligently seek me will find me."

PROVERBS 8:17 NASB

And we have known and believed the love that God has for us. God is love, and he who abides in love abides in God, and God in him. Love has been perfected among us in this: that we may have boldness in the day of judgment; because as He is, so are we in this world. There is no fear in love; but perfect love casts out fear, because fear involves torment. But he who fears has not been made perfect in love. We love Him because He first loved us.

1 JOHN 4:16–19 NKJV

So that Christ may dwell in your hearts through faith; and that you, being rooted and grounded in love, may be able to comprehend with all the saints what is the breadth and length and height and depth, and to know the love of Christ which surpasses knowledge, that you may be filled up to all the fullness of God.

EPHESIANS 3:17–19 NASB

"Those who accept my commandments and obey them are the ones who love me. And because they love me, my Father will love them. And I will love them and reveal myself to each of them."

JOHN 14:21 NLT

Keep yourselves in God's love as you wait for the mercy of our Lord Jesus Christ to bring you to eternal life.

JUDE 1:21 NIV

OBEDIENCE

If ye keep my commandments, ye shall abide in my love; even as I have kept my Father's commandments, and abide in his love.

JOHN 15:10 KJV

The things which you learned and received and heard and saw in me, these do, and the God of peace will be with you.

PHILIPPIANS 4:9 NKJV

Obey your leaders and submit to their authority. They keep watch over you as men who must give an account. Obey them so that their work will be a joy, not a burden, for that would be of no advantage to you.

HEBREWS 13:17 NIV

"Not everyone who says to Me, 'Lord, Lord,' will enter the kingdom of heaven, but he who does the will of My Father who is in heaven will enter."

MATTHEW 7:21 NASB

"If you consent and obey, you will eat the best of the land."

ISAIAH 1:19 NASB

"If they hear and serve Him, they will end their days in prosperity and their years in pleasures."

JOB 36:11 NASB

For the person who keeps all of the laws except one is as guilty as a person who has broken all of God's laws.

JAMES 2:10 NLT

"The LORD your God will make you abound in all the work of your hand, in the fruit of your body, in the increase of your livestock, and in the produce of your land for good. For the LORD will again rejoice over you for good as He rejoiced over your fathers, if you obey the voice of the LORD your God, to keep His commandments and His statutes which are written in this Book of the Law, and if you turn to the LORD your God with all your heart and with all your soul."

DEUTERONOMY 30:9–10 NKJV

Samuel said, "Has the LORD as much delight in burnt offerings and sacrifices as in obeying the voice of the LORD? Behold, to obey is better than sacrifice, and to heed than the fat of rams."

1 SAMUEL 15:22 NASB

Let us hear the conclusion of the whole matter: Fear God and keep His commandments, for this is man's all.

ECCLESIASTES 12:13 NKJV

All the paths of the LORD are mercy and truth unto such as keep his covenant and his testimonies.

PSALM 25:10 KJV

And the world is passing away, and the lust of it; but he who does the will of God abides forever.

1 JOHN 2:17 NKJV

For not the hearers of the law are just in the sight of God, but the doers of the law will be justified.

ROMANS 2:13 NKJV

"Oh, that they had such a heart in them that they would fear Me and always keep all My commandments, that it might be well with them and with their children forever!"

DEUTERONOMY 5:29 NKJV

"Now that you know these things, you will be blessed if you do them."

JOHN 13:17 NIV

My son, do not forget my teaching, but keep my commands in your heart, for they will prolong your life many years and bring you prosperity.

PROVERBS 3:1–2 NIV

Furthermore, we had earthly fathers to discipline us, and we respected them; shall we not much rather be subject to the Father of spirits, and live?

HEBREWS 12:9 NASB

And now, just as you accepted Christ Jesus as your Lord, you must continue to follow him. Let your roots grow down into him, and let your lives be built in him. Then your faith will grow strong in the truth you were taught, and you will overflow with thankfulness.

COLOSSIANS 2:6–7 NLT

Submit yourselves for the Lord's sake to every human institution, whether to a king as the one in authority, or to governors as sent by him for the punishment of evildoers and the praise of those who do right.

1 PETER 2:13–14 NASB

In that I command thee this day to love the LORD thy God, to walk in his ways, and to keep his commandments and his statutes and his judgments, that thou mayest live and multiply: and the LORD thy God shall bless thee in the land whither thou goest to possess it.

DEUTERONOMY 30:16 KJV

But prove yourselves doers of the word, and not merely hearers who delude themselves. For if anyone is a hearer of the word and not a doer, he is like a man who looks at his natural face in a mirror; for once he has looked at himself and gone away, he has immediately forgotten what kind of person he was. But one who looks intently at the perfect law, the law of liberty, and abides by it, not having become a forgetful hearer but an effectual doer, this man will be blessed in what he does.

JAMES 1:22–25 NASB

By this we know that we have come to know Him, if we keep His commandments. The one who says, "I have come to know Him," and does not keep His commandments, is a liar, and the truth is not in him; but whoever keeps His word, in him the love of God has truly been perfected. By this we know that we are in Him: the one who says he abides in Him ought himself to walk in the same manner as He walked.

1 JOHN 2:3–6 NASB

But He said, "More than that, blessed are those who hear
the word of God and keep it!"

LUKE 11:28 NKJV

PATIENCE

He who is slow to anger is better than the mighty, and he
who rules his spirit than he who takes a city.

PROVERBS 16:32 NKJV

And so, having patiently waited, he obtained the promise.

HEBREWS 6:15 NASB

Be still before the LORD and wait patiently for him; do
not fret when men succeed in their ways, when they
carry out their wicked schemes. . . . For evil men will
be cut off, but those who hope in the LORD will inherit
the land.

PSALM 37:7, 9 NIV

Be humble and gentle. Be patient with each other, making
allowance for each other's faults because of your love.

EPHESIANS 4:2 NLT

I waited patiently for the LORD; and He inclined to me, and
heard my cry.

PSALM 40:1 NKJV

The testing of your faith produces endurance. And let endurance have its perfect result, so that you may be perfect and complete, lacking in nothing.

JAMES 1:3–4 NASB

That ye be not slothful, but followers of them who through faith and patience inherit the promises.

HEBREWS 6:12 KJV

This calls for patient endurance on the part of the saints who obey God's commandments and remain faithful to Jesus.

REVELATION 14:12 NIV

Rejoice in our confident hope. Be patient in trouble, and keep on praying.

ROMANS 12:12 NLT

Now we exhort you, brethren, warn those who are unruly, comfort the fainthearted, uphold the weak, be patient with all.

1 THESSALONIANS 5:14 NKJV

The end of a thing is better than its beginning; the patient in spirit is better than the proud in spirit.

ECCLESIASTES 7:8 NKJV

The discretion of a man makes him slow to anger, and his glory is to overlook a transgression.

PROVERBS 19:11 NKJV

People with understanding control their anger; a hot temper shows great foolishness.

PROVERBS 14:29 NLT

Therefore be patient, brethren, until the coming of the Lord. The farmer waits for the precious produce of the soil, being patient about it, until it gets the early and late rains. You too be patient; strengthen your hearts, for the coming of the Lord is near.

JAMES 5:7–8 NASB

Wait on the LORD: be of good courage, and he shall strengthen thine heart: wait, I say, on the LORD.

PSALM 27:14 KJV

PEACE

For the Scriptures say, "If you want to enjoy life and see many happy days, keep your tongue from speaking evil and your lips from telling lies. Turn away from evil and do good. Search for peace, and work to maintain it."

1 PETER 3:10–11 NLT

Be anxious for nothing, but in everything by prayer and supplication, with thanksgiving, let your requests be made known to God; and the peace of God, which surpasses all understanding, will guard your hearts and minds through Christ Jesus.

PHILIPPIANS 4:6-7 NKJV

For the mind set on the flesh is death, but the mind set on the Spirit is life and peace.

ROMANS 8:6 NASB

Consider the blameless, observe the upright; there is a future for the man of peace.

PSALM 37:37 NIV

Peace I leave with you, my peace I give unto you: not as the world giveth, give I unto you. Let not your heart be troubled, neither let it be afraid.

JOHN 14:27 KJV

For the Kingdom of God is not a matter of what we eat or drink, but of living a life of goodness and peace and joy in the Holy Spirit.

ROMANS 14:17 NLT

Be at peace among yourselves.

1 THESSALONIANS 5:13 NKJV

"You will keep him in perfect peace, whose mind is stayed on You, because he trusts in You."

ISAIAH 26:3 NKJV

So then we pursue the things which make for peace and the building up of one another.

ROMANS 14:19 NASB

He who dwells in the shelter of the Most High will abide in the shadow of the Almighty.

PSALM 91:1 NASB

"Let not your heart be troubled; you believe in God, believe also in Me."

JOHN 14:1 NKJV

Therefore, having been justified by faith, we have peace with God through our Lord Jesus Christ.

ROMANS 5:1 NKJV

"Glory to God in the highest, and on earth peace among men with whom He is pleased."

LUKE 2:14 NASB

I will lie down and sleep in peace, for you alone, O LORD, make me dwell in safety.

PSALM 4:8 NIV

Have not I commanded thee? Be strong and of a good courage; be not afraid, neither be thou dismayed: for the LORD thy God is with thee whithersoever thou goest.

JOSHUA 1:9 KJV

[Be] diligent to preserve the unity of the Spirit in the bond of peace.

EPHESIANS 4:3 NASB

Surely He shall deliver you from the snare of the fowler and from the perilous pestilence. He shall cover you with His feathers, and under His wings you shall take refuge; His truth shall be your shield and buckler. You shall not be afraid of the terror by night, nor of the arrow that flies by day, nor of the pestilence that walks in darkness, nor of the destruction that lays waste at noonday.

PSALM 91:3–6 NKJV

Turn from evil and do good; seek peace and pursue it.

PSALM 34:14 NIV

And let the peace of God rule in your hearts, to which also you were called in one body; and be thankful.

COLOSSIANS 3:15 NKJV

Do all that you can to live in peace with everyone.

ROMANS 12:18 NLT

A thousand may fall at your side, and ten thousand at your right hand; but it shall not come near you. Only with your eyes shall you look, and see the reward of the wicked. Because you have made the Lord, who is my refuge, even the Most High, your dwelling place, no evil shall befall you, nor shall any plague come near your dwelling.

PSALM 91:7–10 NKJV

Make every effort to live in peace with all men and to be holy; without holiness no one will see the Lord.

HEBREWS 12:14 NIV

Now the fruit of righteousness is sown in peace by those who make peace.

JAMES 3:18 NKJV

Those who love Your law have great peace, and nothing causes them to stumble.

PSALM 119:165 NASB

Now may the Lord of peace Himself give you peace always in every way. The Lord be with you all.

2 THESSALONIANS 3:16 NKJV

God has called us to peace.

1 CORINTHIANS 7:15 NASB

First of all, then, I urge that entreaties and prayers, petitions and thanksgivings, be made on behalf of all men, for kings and all who are in authority, so that we may lead a tranquil and quiet life in all godliness and dignity.

1 TIMOTHY 2:1–2 NASB

The LORD will give strength to His people; the LORD will bless His people with peace.

PSALM 29:11 NKJV

"Blessed are the peacemakers, for they shall be called sons of God."

MATTHEW 5:9 NASB

Deceit is in the heart of them that imagine evil: but to the counsellors of peace is joy.

PROVERBS 12:20 KJV

PERSEVERANCE

I can do all things through Christ who strengthens me.

PHILIPPIANS 4:13 NKJV

To those who by persistence in doing good seek glory, honor and immortality, he will give eternal life.

ROMANS 2:7 NIV

Yet I am not ashamed, because I know whom I have believed, and am convinced that he is able to guard what I have entrusted to him for that day. What you heard from me, keep as the pattern of sound teaching, with faith and love in Christ Jesus.

2 TIMOTHY 1:12–13 NIV

Then Jesus said to those Jews who believed Him, "If you abide in My word, you are My disciples indeed."

JOHN 8:31 NKJV

Here is the perseverance of the saints who keep the commandments of God and their faith in Jesus.

REVELATION 14:12 NASB

God blesses those who patiently endure testing and temptation. Afterward they will receive the crown of life that God has promised to those who love him.

JAMES 1:12 NLT

You therefore must endure hardship as a good soldier of Jesus Christ.

2 TIMOTHY 2:3 NKJV

Let us hold fast the confession of our hope without wavering, for He who promised is faithful.

HEBREWS 10:23 NASB

Whatever you do, do your work heartily, as for the Lord rather than for men, knowing that from the Lord you will receive the reward of the inheritance. It is the Lord Christ whom you serve.

COLOSSIANS 3:23–24 NASB

And let us not be weary in well doing: for in due season we shall reap, if we faint not.

GALATIANS 6:9 KJV

And not only that, but we also glory in tribulations, knowing that tribulation produces perseverance; and perseverance, character; and character, hope.

ROMANS 5:3–4 NKJV

May the Lord direct your hearts into God's love and Christ's perseverance.

2 THESSALONIANS 3:5 NIV

Therefore we also, since we are surrounded by so great a cloud of witnesses, let us lay aside every weight, and the sin which so easily ensnares us, and let us run with endurance the race that is set before us, looking unto Jesus, the author and finisher of our faith, who for the joy that was set before Him endured the cross, despising the shame, and has sat down at the right hand of the throne of God.

HEBREWS 12:1–2 NKJV

You therefore, beloved, since you know this beforehand, beware lest you also fall from your own steadfastness, being led away with the error of the wicked.

2 PETER 3:17 NKJV

Wherefore take unto you the whole armour of God, that ye may be able to withstand in the evil day, and having done all, to stand.

EPHESIANS 6:13 KJV

For we have become partakers of Christ, if we hold fast the beginning of our assurance firm until the end.

HEBREWS 3:14 NASB

"Those who are victorious will sit with me on my throne, just as I was victorious and sat with my Father on his throne."

REVELATION 3:21 NLT

Everyone who competes in the games exercises self-control in all things. They then do it to receive a perishable wreath, but we an imperishable. Therefore I run in such a way, as not without aim; I box in such a way, as not beating the air; but I discipline my body and make it my slave, so that, after I have preached to others, I myself will not be disqualified.

1 CORINTHIANS 9:25–27 NASB

Stand fast therefore in the liberty by which Christ has made us free, and do not be entangled again with a yoke of bondage.

GALATIANS 5:1 NKJV

I have fought a good fight, I have finished my course, I have kept the faith: Henceforth there is laid up for me a crown of righteousness, which the Lord, the righteous judge, shall give me at that day: and not to me only, but unto all them also that love his appearing.

2 TIMOTHY 4:7–8 KJV

PHYSICAL CARE

And so, dear brothers and sisters, I plead with you to give your bodies to God because of all he has done for you. Let them be a living and holy sacrifice—the kind he will find acceptable. This is truly the way to worship him. Don't copy the behavior and customs of this world, but let God transform you into a new person by changing the way you think. Then you will learn to know God's will for you, which is good and pleasing and perfect. Because of the privilege and authority God has given me, I give each of you this warning: Don't think you are better than you really are. Be honest in your evaluation of yourselves, measuring yourselves by the faith God has given us.

ROMANS 12:1–3 NLT

For bodily discipline is only of little profit, but godliness is profitable for all things, since it holds promise for the present life and also for the life to come.

1 TIMOTHY 4:8 NASB

Do you not know that your body is a temple of the Holy Spirit, who is in you, whom you have received from God? You are not your own; you were bought at a price. Therefore honor God with your body.

1 CORINTHIANS 6:19–20 NIV

Beloved, I pray that in all respects you may prosper and be in good health, just as your soul prospers.

3 JOHN 1:2 NASB

"Do not fear those who kill the body but are unable to kill the soul; but rather fear Him who is able to destroy both soul and body in hell."

MATTHEW 10:28 NASB

Therefore, from now on, we regard no one according to the flesh. Even though we have known Christ according to the flesh, yet now we know Him thus no longer. Therefore, if anyone is in Christ, he is a new creation; old things have passed away; behold, all things have become new.

2 CORINTHIANS 5:16–17 NKJV

You do not know what will happen tomorrow. For what is your life? It is even a vapor that appears for a little time and then vanishes away. Instead you ought to say, "If the Lord wills, we shall live and do this or that."

JAMES 4:14–15 NKJV

Charm is deceitful and beauty is passing, but a woman who fears the LORD, she shall be praised.

PROVERBS 31:30 NKJV

"Do not judge according to appearance, but judge with righteous judgment."

JOHN 7:24 NKJV

But the LORD said unto Samuel, Look not on his countenance, or on the height of his stature; because I have refused him: for the LORD seeth not as man seeth; for man looketh on the outward appearance, but the LORD looketh on the heart.

1 SAMUEL 16:7 KJV

Likewise, I want women to adorn themselves with proper clothing, modestly and discreetly, not with braided hair and gold or pearls or costly garments, but rather by means of good works, as is proper for women making a claim to godliness.

1 TIMOTHY 2:9–10 NASB

If you show special attention to the man wearing fine clothes and say, "Here's a good seat for you," but say to the poor man, "You stand there" or "Sit on the floor by my feet," have you not discriminated among yourselves and become judges with evil thoughts?

JAMES 2:3–4 NIV

PRAYER

Therefore I want the men in every place to pray, lifting up holy hands, without wrath and dissension.

1 TIMOTHY 2:8 NASB

"If you sinful people know how to give good gifts to your children, how much more will your heavenly Father give good gifts to those who ask him."

MATTHEW 7:11 NLT

In the same way the Spirit also helps our weakness; for we do not know how to pray as we should, but the Spirit Himself intercedes for us with groanings too deep for words.

ROMANS 8:26 NASB

The LORD is near to all who call upon Him, to all who call upon Him in truth.

PSALM 145:18 NKJV

Then shall ye call upon me, and ye shall go and pray unto me, and I will hearken unto you.

JEREMIAH 29:12 KJV

He shall call upon Me, and I will answer him; I will be with him in trouble; I will deliver him and honor him.

PSALM 91:15 NKJV

You will make your prayer to Him, He will hear you, and you will pay your vows.

JOB 22:27 NKJV

"Until now you have asked for nothing in My name; ask and you will receive, so that your joy may be made full."

JOHN 16:24 NASB

The LORD detests the sacrifice of the wicked, but the prayer of the upright pleases him.

PROVERBS 15:8 NIV

Be anxious for nothing, but in everything by prayer and supplication with thanksgiving let your requests be made known to God. And the peace of God, which surpasses all comprehension, will guard your hearts and your minds in Christ Jesus.

PHILIPPIANS 4:6–7 NASB

"We will give ourselves continually to prayer and to the ministry of the word."

ACTS 6:4 NKJV

"It will also come to pass that before they call, I will answer; and while they are still speaking, I will hear."

ISAIAH 65:24 NASB

For the people shall dwell in Zion at Jerusalem; you shall weep no more. He will be very gracious to you at the sound of your cry; when He hears it, He will answer you.

ISAIAH 30:19 NKJV

Morning, noon, and night I cry out in my distress, and the LORD hears my voice.

PSALM 55:17 NLT

"Ask, and it will be given to you; seek, and you will find; knock, and it will be opened to you."

MATTHEW 7:7 NKJV

"Again I say to you that if two of you agree on earth concerning anything that they ask, it will be done for them by My Father in heaven. For where two or three are gathered together in My name, I am there in the midst of them."

MATTHEW 18:19–20 NKJV

For this shall every one that is godly pray unto thee in a time when thou mayest be found: surely in the floods of great waters they shall not come nigh unto him.

PSALM 32:6 KJV

Therefore, confess your sins to one another, and pray for one another so that you may be healed. The effective prayer of a righteous man can accomplish much.

JAMES 5:16 NASB

But I pray to you, O LORD, in the time of your favor; in your great love, O God, answer me with your sure salvation.

PSALM 69:13 NIV

Praying always with all prayer and supplication in the Spirit, being watchful to this end with all perseverance and supplication for all the saints.

EPHESIANS 6:18 NKJV

Rejoicing in hope, persevering in tribulation, devoted to prayer. . .

ROMANS 12:12 NASB

"Then he will pray to God, and He will accept him, that he may see His face with joy, and He may restore His righteousness to man."

JOB 33:26 NASB

O LORD, hear me as I pray; pay attention to my groaning. Listen to my cry for help, my King and my God, for I pray to no one but you. Listen to my voice in the morning, LORD.

PSALM 5:1–3 NLT

I waited patiently for the LORD; and he inclined unto me, and heard my cry.

PSALM 40:1 KJV

"But when you pray, go away by yourself, shut the door behind you, and pray to your Father in private. Then your Father, who sees everything will reward you. When you pray, don't babble on and on as people of other religions do. They think their prayers are answered merely by repeating their words again and again."

MATTHEW 6:6–7 NLT

What is the outcome then? I will pray with the spirit and I will pray with the mind also; I will sing with the spirit and I will sing with the mind also.

1 CORINTHIANS 14:15 NASB

Let us then approach the throne of grace with confidence, so that we may receive mercy and find grace to help us in our time of need.

HEBREWS 4:16 NIV

The prayer offered in faith will restore the one who is sick, and the Lord will raise him up, and if he has committed sins, they will be forgiven him.

JAMES 5:15 NASB

"And whatever things you ask in prayer, believing, you will receive."

MATTHEW 21:22 NKJV

Pray without ceasing; in everything give thanks; for this is God's will for you in Christ Jesus.

1 THESSALONIANS 5:17–18 NASB

Now this is the confidence that we have in Him, that if we ask anything according to His will, He hears us. And if we know that He hears us, whatever we ask, we know that we have the petitions that we have asked of Him.

1 JOHN 5:14–15 NKJV

If my people, which are called by my name, shall humble themselves, and pray, and seek my face, and turn from their wicked ways; then will I hear from heaven, and will forgive their sin, and will heal their land.

2 CHRONICLES 7:14 KJV

PURITY

So I say, let the Holy Spirit guide your lives. Then you won't be doing what your sinful nature craves.

GALATIANS 5:16 NLT

The body is not meant for sexual immorality, but for the Lord, and the Lord for the body.

1 CORINTHIANS 6:13 NIV

For all that is in the world—the lust of the flesh, the lust of the eyes, and the pride of life—is not of the Father but is of the world. And the world is passing away, and the lust of it; but he who does the will of God abides forever.

1 JOHN 2:16–17 NKJV

But I say unto you, That whosoever looketh on a woman to lust after her hath committed adultery with her already in his heart.

MATTHEW 5:28 KJV

Now concerning the things about which you wrote, it is good for a man not to touch a woman. But because of immoralities, each man is to have his own wife, and each woman is to have her own husband.

1 CORINTHIANS 7:1–2 NASB

Be imitators of God, therefore, as dearly loved children and live a life of love, just as Christ loved us and gave himself up for us as a fragrant offering and sacrifice to God. But among you there must not be even a hint of sexual immorality, or of any kind of impurity, or of greed, because these are improper for God's holy people.

EPHESIANS 5:1–3 NIV

Now those who belong to Christ Jesus have crucified the flesh with its passions and desires.

GALATIANS 5:24 NASB

But put on the Lord Jesus Christ, and make no provision for the flesh, to fulfill its lusts.

ROMANS 13:14 NKJV

For this is the will of God, your sanctification: that you should abstain from sexual immorality; that each of you should know how to possess his own vessel in sanctification and honor, not in passion of lust, like the Gentiles who do not know God. . .for God did not call us to uncleanness, but in holiness.

1 THESSALONIANS 4:3–5, 7 NKJV

"I have made a covenant with my eyes; why then should I look upon a young woman?"

JOB 31:1 NKJV

Therefore put to death your members which are on the earth: fornication, uncleanness, passion, evil desire, and covetousness, which is idolatry. Because of these things the wrath of God is coming upon the sons of disobedience.

COLOSSIANS 3:5–6 NKJV

Finally, brethren, whatever is true, whatever is honorable, whatever is right, whatever is pure, whatever is lovely, whatever is of good repute, if there is any excellence and if anything worthy of praise, dwell on these things.

PHILIPPIANS 4:8 NASB

RELATIONSHIPS

Now may the God who gives perseverance and encouragement grant you to be of the same mind with one another according to Christ Jesus.

ROMANS 15:5 NASB

"Honor your father and mother." This is the first commandment with a promise. If you honor your father and mother, "things will go well for you, and you will have a long life on the earth."

EPHESIANS 6:2–3 NLT

Be subject to one another in the fear of Christ.

EPHESIANS 5:21 NASB

For all the law is fulfilled in one word, even in this: *"You shall love your neighbor as yourself."*

GALATIANS 5:14 NKJV

Finally, all of you, live in harmony with one another; be sympathetic, love as brothers, be compassionate and humble.

1 PETER 3:8 NIV

If you really fulfill the royal law according to the Scripture, *"You shall love your neighbor as yourself,"* you do well.

JAMES 2:8 NKJV

Anyone who hates his brother is a murderer, and you know that no murderer has eternal life in him.

1 JOHN 3:15 NIV

"You shall not take vengeance, nor bear any grudge against the sons of your people, but you shall love your neighbor as yourself; I am the LORD."

LEVITICUS 19:18 NASB

So speak and so do as those who will be judged by the law of liberty. For judgment is without mercy to the one who has shown no mercy. Mercy triumphs over judgment.

JAMES 2:12–13 NKJV

Though I speak with the tongues of men and of angels, and have not charity, I am become as sounding brass, or a tinkling cymbal. And though I have the gift of prophecy, and understand all mysteries, and all knowledge; and though I have all faith, so that I could remove mountains, and have not charity, I am nothing. And though I bestow all my goods to feed the poor, and though I give my body to be burned, and have not charity, it profiteth me nothing.

1 CORINTHIANS 13:1–3 KJV

Beloved, let us love one another: for love is of God; and every one that loveth is born of God, and knoweth God.

1 JOHN 4:7 KJV

Owe nothing to anyone except to love one another; for he who loves his neighbor has fulfilled the law.

ROMANS 13:8 NASB

Be happy with those who are happy, and weep with those who weep.

ROMANS 12:15 NLT

Now the fruit of righteousness is sown in peace by those who make peace.

JAMES 3:18 NKJV

"But love your enemies, do good, and lend, hoping for nothing in return; and your reward will be great, and you will be sons of the Most High. For He is kind to the unthankful and evil. Therefore be merciful, just as your Father also is merciful."

LUKE 6:35–36 NKJV

Bear one another's burdens, and thereby fulfill the law of Christ.

GALATIANS 6:2 NASB

"You have heard that it was said, 'YOU SHALL LOVE YOUR NEIGHBOR and hate your enemy.' But I say to you, love your enemies and pray for those who persecute you, so that you may be sons of your Father who is in heaven; for He causes His sun to rise on the evil and the good, and sends rain on the righteous and the unrighteous."

MATTHEW 5:43–45 NASB

For this is the message which you have heard from the beginning, that we should love one another.

1 JOHN 3:11 NASB

Be kindly affectioned one to another with brotherly love; in honour preferring one another.

ROMANS 12:10 KJV

"Therefore, if you are offering your gift at the altar and there remember that your brother has something against you, leave your gift there in front of the altar. First go and be reconciled to your brother; then come and offer your gift."

MATTHEW 5:23–24 NIV

Honor all people. Love the brotherhood. Fear God. Honor the king.

1 PETER 2:17 NKJV

Beloved, if God so loved us, we also ought to love one another. No one has seen God at any time. If we love one another, God abides in us, and His love has been perfected in us.

1 JOHN 4:11–12 NKJV

"This is My commandment, that you love one another as I have loved you. Greater love has no one than this, than to lay down one's life for his friends."

JOHN 15:12–13 NKJV

Love is patient, love is kind and is not jealous; love does not brag and is not arrogant, does not act unbecomingly; it does not seek its own, is not provoked, does not take into account a wrong suffered.

1 CORINTHIANS 13:4–5 NASB

Don't team up with those who are unbelievers. How can righteousness be a partner with wickedness? How can light live with darkness?

2 CORINTHIANS 6:14 NLT

REPENTANCE

"So remember what you have received and heard; and keep it, and repent. Therefore if you do not wake up, I will come like a thief, and you will not know at what hour I will come to you."

REVELATION 3:3 NASB

Therefore, confess your sins to one another, and pray for one another so that you may be healed. The effective prayer of a righteous man can accomplish much.

JAMES 5:16 NASB

"But go and learn what this means: 'I desire mercy, not sacrifice.' For I have not come to call the righteous, but sinners."

MATTHEW 9:13 NIV

"If you return to the Almighty, you will be restored; if you remove unrighteousness far from your tent."

JOB 22:23 NASB

Wherefore I say unto you, All manner of sin and blasphemy shall be forgiven unto men: but the blasphemy against the Holy Ghost shall not be forgiven unto men.

MATTHEW 12:31 KJV

The sacrifices of God are a broken spirit, a broken and a contrite heart—these, O God, You will not despise.

PSALM 51:17 NKJV

"But if wicked people turn away from all their sins and begin to obey my decrees and do what is just and right, they will surely live and not die. All their past sins will be forgotten, and they will live because of the righteous things they have done. Do you think that I like to see wicked people die?" says the Sovereign LORD. "Of course not! I want them to turn from their wicked ways and live."

EZEKIEL 18:21–23 NLT

The LORD has heard my supplication; the LORD will receive my prayer.

PSALM 6:9 NKJV

Draw near to God and He will draw near to you. Cleanse your hands, you sinners; and purify your hearts, you double-minded.

JAMES 4:8 NKJV

"God. . .commands all people everywhere to repent."

ACTS 17:30 NIV

Or do you think lightly of the riches of His kindness and tolerance and patience, not knowing that the kindness of God leads you to repentance?

ROMANS 2:4 NASB

The LORD is close to the brokenhearted; he rescues those whose spirits are crushed.

PSALM 34:18 NLT

He who conceals his transgressions will not prosper, but he who confesses and forsakes them will find compassion.

PROVERBS 28:13 NASB

Seek the LORD while He may be found, call upon Him while He is near. Let the wicked forsake his way, and the unrighteous man his thoughts; let him return to the LORD, and He will have mercy on him; and to our God, for He will abundantly pardon.

ISAIAH 55:6–7 NKJV

If we confess our sins, He is faithful and just to forgive us our sins and to cleanse us from all unrighteousness.

1 JOHN 1:9 NKJV

For they themselves report about us what kind of a reception we had with you, and how you turned to God from idols to serve a living and true God, and to wait for His Son from heaven, whom He raised from the dead, that is Jesus, who rescues us from the wrath to come.

1 THESSALONIANS 1:9–10 NASB

"Therefore repent of this wickedness of yours, and pray the Lord that, if possible, the intention of your heart may be forgiven you."

ACTS 8:22 NASB

I acknowledged my sin to You, and my iniquity I have not hidden. I said, "I will confess my transgressions to the LORD," and You forgave the iniquity of my sin.

PSALM 32:5 NKJV

"Then he will pray to God, and He will accept him, that he may see His face with joy, and He may restore His righteousness to man."

JOB 33:26 NASB

Repent ye therefore, and be converted, that your sins may be blotted out, when the times of refreshing shall come from the presence of the Lord.

ACTS 3:19 KJV

"But at last my people will confess their sins and the sins of their ancestors for betraying me and being hostile toward me. When I have turned their hostility back on them and have brought them to the land of their enemies, then at last their stubborn hearts will be humbled, and they will pay for their sins. Then I will remember my covenant with Jacob, and my covenant with Isaac and my covenant with Abraham, and I will remember the land."

LEVITICUS 26:40–42 NLT

"The time is fulfilled, and the kingdom of God is at hand; repent and believe in the gospel."

MARK 1:15 NASB

"Repent, for the kingdom of heaven is at hand!"

MATTHEW 3:2 NKJV

And rend your heart, and not your garments, and turn unto the LORD your God: for he is gracious and merciful, slow to anger, and of great kindness, and repenteth him of the evil.

JOEL 2:13 KJV

"In the same way, I tell you, there is rejoicing in the presence of the angels of God over one sinner who repents."

LUKE 15:10 NIV

Who may ascend into the hill of the LORD? Or who may stand in His holy place? He who has clean hands and a pure heart, who has not lifted up his soul to an idol, nor sworn deceitfully. He shall receive blessing from the LORD, and righteousness from the God of his salvation.

PSALM 24:3–5 NKJV

Speak unto the children of Israel, When a man or woman shall commit any sin that men commit, to do a trespass against the LORD, and that person be guilty; then they shall confess their sin which they have done: and he shall recompense his trespass with the principal thereof, and add unto it the fifth part thereof, and give it unto him against whom he hath trespassed.

NUMBERS 5:6–7 KJV

RESPONSIBILITY

And they were both righteous before God, walking in all the commandments and ordinances of the Lord blameless.

LUKE 1:6 NKJV

But let each one examine his own work, and then he will have rejoicing in himself alone, and not in another. For each one shall bear his own load.

GALATIANS 6:4–5 NKJV

Do everything without complaining and arguing, so that no one can criticize you. Live clean, innocent lives as children of God, shining like bright lights in a world full of crooked and perverse people. Hold firmly to the word of life; then, on the day of Christ's return, I will be proud that I did not run the race in vain and that my work was not useless.

PHILIPPIANS 2:14–16 NLT

"Therefore I will judge you, O house of Israel, each according to his conduct," declares the Lord GOD. "Repent and turn away from all your transgressions, so that iniquity may not become a stumbling block to you."

EZEKIEL 18:30 NASB

"I will give to each one of you according to your deeds."

REVELATION 2:23 NASB

RIGHTEOUSNESS

And it shall come to pass, if thou shalt hearken diligently unto the voice of the LORD thy God, to observe and to do all his commandments which I command thee this day, that the LORD thy God will set thee on high above all nations of the earth.

DEUTERONOMY 28:1 KJV

Ye that love the LORD, hate evil: he preserveth the souls of his saints; he delivereth them out of the hand of the wicked. Light is sown for the righteous.

PSALM 97:10–11 KJV

Then shall thy light break forth as the morning, and thine health shall spring forth speedily: and thy righteousness shall go before thee; the glory of the LORD shall be thy reward.

ISAIAH 58:8 KJV

Thy word is true from the beginning: and every one of thy righteous judgments endureth for ever.

PSALM 119:160 KJV

The righteous cry, and the LORD heareth, and delivereth them out of all their troubles.

PSALM 34:17 KJV

Lord, who shall abide in thy tabernacle? who shall dwell in thy holy hill? He that walketh uprightly, and worketh righteousness, and speaketh the truth in his heart.

PSALM 15:1–2 KJV

Then shall the righteous shine forth as the sun in the kingdom of their Father. Who hath ears to hear, let him hear.

MATTHEW 13:43 KJV

That ye may be blameless and harmless, the sons of God, without rebuke, in the midst of a crooked and perverse nation, among whom ye shine as lights in the world.

PHILIPPIANS 2:15 KJV

Whereby are given unto us exceeding great and precious promises: that by these ye might be partakers of the divine nature, having escaped the corruption that is in the world through lust.

2 PETER 1:4 KJV

But if thou shalt indeed obey his voice, and do all that I speak; then I will be an enemy unto thine enemies, and an adversary unto thine adversaries.

EXODUS 23:22 KJV

If we confess our sins, he is faithful and just to forgive us our sins, and to cleanse us from all unrighteousness.

1 JOHN 1:9 KJV

The eyes of the LORD are upon the righteous, and his ears are open unto their cry.

PSALM 34:15 KJV

The LORD will not suffer the soul of the righteous to famish: but he casteth away the substance of the wicked.

PROVERBS 10:3 KJV

But know that the LORD hath set apart him that is godly for himself: the LORD will hear when I call unto him.

PSALM 4:3 KJV

He that followeth after righteousness and mercy findeth life, righteousness, and honour.

PROVERBS 21:21 KJV

The righteous shall be glad in the LORD, and shall trust in him; and all the upright in heart shall glory.

PSALM 64:10 KJV

Blessed are they which do hunger and thirst after righteousness: for they shall be filled.

MATTHEW 5:6 KJV

A righteous man hateth lying: but a wicked man is loathsome, and cometh to shame.

PROVERBS 13:5 KJV

Blessed are they which are persecuted for righteousness' sake: for theirs is the kingdom of heaven.

MATTHEW 5:10 KJV

Know ye not that the unrighteous shall not inherit the kingdom of God? Be not deceived.

1 CORINTHIANS 6:9 KJV

Then shall he answer them, saying, Verily I say unto you, Inasmuch as ye did it not to one of the least of these, ye did it not to me. And these shall go away into everlasting punishment: but the righteous into life eternal.

Matthew 25:45–46 KJV

Salvation

Jesus answered and said to him, "Truly, truly, I say to you, unless one is born again he cannot see the kingdom of God." Nicodemus said to Him, "How can a man be born when he is old? He cannot enter a second time into his mother's womb and be born, can he?" Jesus answered, "Truly, truly, I say to you, unless one is born of water and the Spirit he cannot enter into the kingdom of God. That which is born of the flesh is flesh, and that which is born of the Spirit is spirit. Do not be amazed that I said to you, 'You must be born again.'"

John 3:3–7 NASB

For by grace you have been saved through faith, and that not of yourselves; it is the gift of God.

Ephesians 2:8 NKJV

"Therefore let it be known to you, brethren, that through Him forgiveness of sins is proclaimed to you."

Acts 13:38 NASB

My dear children, I am writing this to you so that you will not sin. But if anyone does sin, we have an advocate who pleads our case before the Father. He is Jesus Christ, the one who is truly righteous. He himself is the sacrifice that atones for our sins—and not only our sins but the sins of all the world.

1 JOHN 2:1–2 NLT

"I am the door; if anyone enters through Me, he will be saved, and will go in and out and find pasture."

JOHN 10:9 NASB

If you confess with your mouth Jesus as Lord, and believe in your heart that God raised Him from the dead, you will be saved; for with the heart a person believes, resulting in righteousness, and with the mouth he confesses, resulting in salvation. For the Scripture says, "WHOEVER BELIEVES IN HIM WILL NOT BE DISAPPOINTED." For there is no distinction between Jew and Greek; for the same Lord is Lord of all, abounding in riches for all who call on Him; for "WHOEVER WILL CALL ON THE NAME OF THE LORD WILL BE SAVED."

ROMANS 10:9–13 NASB

"Look! I stand at the door and knock. If you hear my voice and open the door, I will come in, and we will share a meal together as friends."

REVELATION 3:20 NLT

"He who believes and is baptized will be saved; but he who does not believe will be condemned."

MARK 16:16 NKJV

But to all who believed him and accepted him, he gave the right to become children of God. They are reborn—not with a physical birth resulting from human passion or plan, but a birth that comes from God.

JOHN 1:12–13 NLT

For this is good and acceptable in the sight of God our Savior, who desires all men to be saved and to come to the knowledge of the truth.

1 TIMOTHY 2:3–4 NKJV

"He who believes in Him is not condemned; but he who does not believe is condemned already, because he has not believed in the name of the only begotten Son of God."

JOHN 3:18 NKJV

God made him who had no sin to be sin for us, so that in him we might become the righteousness of God.

2 CORINTHIANS 5:21 NIV

"I give eternal life to them, and they will never perish; and no one will snatch them out of My hand."

JOHN 10:28 NASB

"I tell you that in the same way, there will be more joy in heaven over one sinner who repents than over ninety-nine righteous persons who need no repentance."

LUKE 15:7 NASB

"Nor is there salvation in any other, for there is no other name under heaven given among men by which we must be saved."

ACTS 4:12 NKJV

But when the kindness and the love of God our Savior toward man appeared, not by works of righteousness which we have done, but according to His mercy He saved us, through the washing of regeneration and renewing of the Holy Spirit, whom He poured out on us abundantly through Jesus Christ our Savior.

TITUS 3:4–6 NKJV

And they said, Believe on the Lord Jesus Christ, and thou shalt be saved, and thy house.

ACTS 16:31 KJV

"Enter through the narrow gate. For wide is the gate and broad is the road that leads to destruction, and many enter through it. But small is the gate and narrow the road that leads to life, and only a few find it."

MATTHEW 7:13–14 NIV

"He who believes in the Son has eternal life; but he who does not obey the Son will not see life, but the wrath of God abides on him."

JOHN 3:36 NASB

Therefore, if anyone is in Christ, he is a new creation; old things have passed away; behold, all things have become new.

2 CORINTHIANS 5:17 NKJV

Therefore lay aside all filthiness and overflow of wickedness, and receive with meekness the implanted word, which is able to save your souls.

JAMES 1:21 NKJV

SCRIPTURE

Let the word of Christ richly dwell within you, with all wisdom teaching and admonishing one another with psalms and hymns and spiritual songs, singing with thankfulness in your hearts to God.

COLOSSIANS 3:16 NASB

You should remember the words spoken beforehand by the holy prophets and the commandment of the Lord and Savior spoken by your apostles.

2 PETER 3:2 NASB

I have hidden your word in my heart, that I might not sin against you.

PSALM 119:11 NLT

"As for God, His way is blameless; the word of the LORD is tested; He is a shield to all who take refuge in Him."

2 SAMUEL 22:31 NASB

But you must continue in the things which you have learned and been assured of, knowing from whom you have learned them, and that from childhood you have known the Holy Scriptures, which are able to make you wise for salvation through faith which is in Christ Jesus.

2 TIMOTHY 3:14–15 NKJV

So shall my word be that goeth forth out of my mouth: it shall not return unto me void, but it shall accomplish that which I please, and it shall prosper in the thing whereto I sent it.

ISAIAH 55:11 KJV

For the word of God is living and powerful, and sharper than any two-edged sword, piercing even to the division of soul and spirit, and of joints and marrow, and is a discerner of the thoughts and intents of the heart.

HEBREWS 4:12 NKJV

Your word is a lamp to my feet and a light for my path.

PSALM 119:105 NIV

My son, give attention to my words; incline your ear to my sayings. Do not let them depart from your eyes; keep them in the midst of your heart; for they are life to those who find them, and health to all their flesh.

PROVERBS 4:20–22 NKJV

The statutes of the LORD are right, rejoicing the heart; the commandment of the LORD is pure, enlightening the eyes.

PSALM 19:8 NKJV

Seek ye out of the book of the LORD, and read: no one of these shall fail, none shall want her mate: for my mouth it hath commanded, and his spirit it hath gathered them.

ISAIAH 34:16 KJV

All Scripture is inspired by God and profitable for teaching, for reproof, for correction, for training in righteousness; so that the man of God may be adequate, equipped for every good work.

2 TIMOTHY 3:16–17 NASB

Forever, O LORD, Your word is settled in heaven.

PSALM 119:89 NKJV

But know this first of all, that no prophecy of Scripture is a matter of one's own interpretation, for no prophecy was ever made by an act of human will, but men moved by the Holy Spirit spoke from God.

2 PETER 1:20–21 NASB

"Do not let this Book of the Law depart from your mouth; meditate on it day and night, so that you may be careful to do everything written in it. Then you will be prosperous and successful."

JOSHUA 1:8 NIV

"So commit yourselves wholeheartedly to these words of mine. Tie them to your hands and wear them on your forehead as reminders. Teach them to your children. Talk about them when you are at home and when you are on the road, when you are going to bed and when you are getting up again."

DEUTERONOMY 11:18–19 NLT

SELF-CONTROL

Or do you not know that the unrighteous will not inherit the kingdom of God? Do not be deceived; neither fornicators, nor idolaters, nor adulterers, nor effeminate, nor homosexuals, nor thieves, nor the covetous, nor drunkards, nor revilers, nor swindlers, will inherit the kingdom of God. Such were some of you; but you were washed, but you were sanctified, but you were justified in the name of the Lord Jesus Christ and in the Spirit of our God.

1 CORINTHIANS 6:9-11 NASB

For the grace of God that bringeth salvation hath appeared to all men, teaching us that, denying ungodliness and worldly lusts, we should live soberly, righteously, and godly, in this present world; looking for that blessed hope, and the glorious appearing of the great God and our Saviour Jesus Christ; who gave himself for us, that he might redeem us from all iniquity, and purify unto himself a peculiar people, zealous of good works.

TITUS 2:11–14 KJV

Whoever has no rule over his own spirit is like a city broken down, without walls.

PROVERBS 25:28 NKJV

Therefore, dear brothers and sisters, you have no obligation to do what your sinful nature urges you to do. For if you live by its dictates, you will die. But if through the power of the Spirit you put to death the deeds of your sinful nature, you will live.

ROMANS 8:12-13 NLT

For you have been called for this purpose, since Christ also suffered for you, leaving you an example for you to follow in His steps, WHO COMMITTED NO SIN, NOR WAS ANY DECEIT FOUND IN HIS MOUTH; and while being reviled, He did not revile in return; while suffering, He uttered no threats, but kept entrusting Himself to Him who judges righteously.

1 PETER 2:21–23 NASB

But also for this very reason, giving all diligence, add to your faith virtue, to virtue knowledge, to knowledge self-control, to self-control perseverance, to perseverance godliness, to godliness brotherly kindness, and to brotherly kindness love. For if these things are yours and abound, you will be neither barren nor unfruitful in the knowledge of our Lord Jesus Christ.

2 PETER 1:5–8 NKJV

Let your gentleness be known to all men. The Lord is at hand.

PHILIPPIANS 4:5 NKJV

SIN

He has removed our sins as far from us as the east is from the west.

PSALM 103:12 NLT

My dear children, I write this to you so that you will not sin. But if anybody does sin, we have one who speaks to the Father in our defense—Jesus Christ, the Righteous One. He is the atoning sacrifice for our sins, and not only for ours but also for the sins of the whole world.

1 JOHN 2:1-2 NIV

This is a faithful saying and worthy of all acceptance, that Christ Jesus came into the world to save sinners, of whom I am chief.

1 TIMOTHY 1:15 NKJV

Our old self was crucified with Him, in order that our body of sin might be done away with, so that we would no longer be slaves to sin; for he who has died is freed from sin.

ROMANS 6:6–7 NASB

Grace and peace to you from God our Father and the Lord Jesus Christ, who gave himself for our sins to rescue us from the present evil age, according to the will of our God and Father.

GALATIANS 1:3–4 NIV

Who Himself bore our sins in His own body on the tree, that we, having died to sins, might live for righteousness—by whose stripes you were healed.

1 PETER 2:24 NKJV

"Of Him all the prophets bear witness that through His name everyone who believes in Him receives forgiveness of sins."

ACTS 10:43 NASB

Your eyes are too pure to approve evil, and You can not look on wickedness with favor. Why do You look with favor on those who deal treacherously? Why are You silent when the wicked swallow up those more righteous than they?

HABAKKUK 1:13 NASB

"Come now, and let us reason together," says the LORD, "though your sins are like scarlet, they shall be as white as snow; though they are red like crimson, they shall be as wool."

ISAIAH 1:18 NKJV

But he was wounded for our transgressions, he was bruised for our iniquities: the chastisement of our peace was upon him; and with his stripes we are healed. All we like sheep have gone astray; we have turned every one to his own way; and the LORD hath laid on him the iniquity of us all.

ISAIAH 53:5–6 KJV

"For I will be merciful to their unrighteousness, and their sins and their lawless deeds I will remember no more."

HEBREWS 8:12 NKJV

God's law was given so that all people could see how sinful they were. But as people sinned more and more, God's wonderful grace became more abundant.

ROMANS 5:20 NLT

If we walk in the Light as He Himself is in the Light, we have fellowship with one another, and the blood of Jesus His Son cleanses us from all sin.

1 JOHN 1:7 NASB

SOBRIETY

Wine is a mocker, strong drink a brawler, and whoever is intoxicated by it is not wise.

PROVERBS 20:1 NASB

Do not be with heavy drinkers of wine, or with gluttonous eaters of meat. . . . Do not look on the wine when it is red, when it sparkles in the cup, when it goes down smoothly; at the last it bites like a serpent and stings like a viper.

PROVERBS 23:20, 31–32 NASB

Woe unto them that are mighty to drink wine, and men of strength to mingle strong drink.

ISAIAH 5:22 KJV

So whether you eat or drink or whatever you do, do it all for the glory of God.

1 CORINTHIANS 10:31 NIV

They will eat, but not have enough; they will play the harlot, but not increase, because they have stopped giving heed to the LORD. Harlotry, wine and new wine take away the understanding.

HOSEA 4:10–11 NASB

Like tangled thorns, and like those who are drunken with their drink, they are consumed as stubble completely withered.

NAHUM 1:10 NASB

"Now therefore, be careful not to drink wine or strong drink, nor eat any unclean thing."

JUDGES 13:4 NASB

Be sober, be vigilant; because your adversary the devil walks about like a roaring lion, seeking whom he may devour.

1 PETER 5:8 NKJV

Let us walk properly, as in the day, not in revelry and drunkenness, not in lewdness and lust, not in strife and envy.

ROMANS 13:13 NKJV

Who has woe? Who has sorrow? Who has contentions? Who has complaining? Who has wounds without cause? Who has redness of eyes? Those who linger long over wine, those who go to taste mixed wine.

PROVERBS 23:29–30 NASB

Therefore let us not sleep, as others do, but let us watch and be sober. For those who sleep, sleep at night, and those who get drunk are drunk at night.

1 THESSALONIANS 5:6–7 NKJV

Don't be drunk with wine, because that will ruin your life. Instead, be filled with the Holy Spirit singing psalms and hymns and spiritual songs among yourselves, and making music to the Lord in your hearts. And give thanks for everything to God the Father in the name of our Lord Jesus Christ.

EPHESIANS 5:18–20 NLT

The acts of the sinful nature are obvious: sexual immorality, impurity and debauchery; idolatry and witchcraft; hatred, discord, jealousy, fits of rage, selfish ambition, dissensions, factions and envy; drunkenness, orgies, and the like. I warn you, as I did before, that those who live like this will not inherit the kingdom of God.

GALATIANS 5:19–21 NIV

Do you not know that you are the temple of God and that the Spirit of God dwells in you? If anyone defiles the temple of God, God will destroy him. For the temple of God is holy, which temple you are.

1 CORINTHIANS 3:16–17 NKJV

Woe to those who rise early in the morning, that they may follow intoxicating drink; who continue until night, till wine inflames them!

ISAIAH 5:11 NKJV

"But take heed to yourselves, lest your hearts be weighed down with carousing, drunkenness, and cares of this life, and that Day come on you unexpectedly."

LUKE 21:34 NKJV

It is good neither to eat flesh, nor to drink wine, nor any thing whereby thy brother stumbleth, or is offended, or is made weak.

ROMANS 14:21 KJV

For the grace of God that brings salvation has appeared to all men, teaching us that, denying ungodliness and worldly lusts, we should live soberly, righteously, and godly in the present age, looking for the blessed hope and glorious appearing of our great God and Savior Jesus Christ.

TITUS 2:11–13 NKJV

"What sorrow awaits you who make your neighbors drunk! You force your cup on them so you can gloat over their shameful nakedness."

HABAKKUK 2:15 NLT

For the heavy drinker and the glutton will come to poverty, and drowsiness will clothe one with rags.

PROVERBS 23:21 NASB

You are all sons of light and sons of day. We are not of night nor of darkness; so then let us not sleep as others do, but let us be alert and sober.

1 THESSALONIANS 5:5–6 NASB

TEMPTATION

For we do not have a high priest who cannot sympathize with our weaknesses, but One who has been tempted in all things as we are, yet without sin. Therefore let us draw near with confidence to the throne of grace, so that we may receive mercy and find grace to help in time of need.

HEBREWS 4:15–16 NASB

When He came to the place, He said to them, "Pray that you may not enter into temptation."

LUKE 22:40 NKJV

Though he fall, he shall not be utterly cast down: for the LORD upholdeth him with his hand.

PSALM 37:24 KJV

"And do not lead us into temptation, but deliver us from evil. [For Yours is the kingdom and the power and the glory forever. Amen.]"

MATTHEW 6:13 NASB

Great peace have those who love Your law, and nothing causes them to stumble.

PSALM 119:165 NKJV

"Watch and pray so that you will not fall into temptation. The spirit is willing, but the body is weak."

MATTHEW 26:41 NIV

Blessed is a man who perseveres under trial; for once he has been approved, he will receive the crown of life which the Lord has promised to those who love Him. Let no one say when he is tempted, "I am being tempted by God"; for God cannot be tempted by evil, and He Himself does not tempt anyone. But each one is tempted when he is carried away and enticed by his own lust. Then when lust has conceived, it gives birth to sin; and when sin is accomplished, it brings forth death.

JAMES 1:12–15 NASB

Therefore let him who thinks he stands take heed that he does not fall. No temptation has overtaken you but such as is common to man; and God is faithful, who will not allow you to be tempted beyond what you are able, but with the temptation will provide the way of escape also, so that you will be able to endure it.

1 CORINTHIANS 10:12–13 NASB

So you see, the Lord knows how to rescue godly people from their trials, even while keeping the wicked under punishment until the day of final judgment.

2 PETER 2:9 NLT

THOUGHT LIFE

Do not conform any longer to the pattern of this world, but be transformed by the renewing of your mind. Then you will be able to test and approve what God's will is—his good, pleasing and perfect will.

ROMANS 12:2 NIV

"The good man brings good things out of the good stored up in his heart, and the evil man brings evil things out of the evil stored up in his heart. For out of the overflow of his heart his mouth speaks."

LUKE 6:45 NIV

I remember the days of old; I meditate on all Your works; I muse on the work of Your hands.

PSALM 143:5 NKJV

Evil plans are an abomination to the LORD, but pleasant words are pure.

PROVERBS 15:26 NASB

"I, the LORD, search the heart, I test the mind, even to give to each man according to his ways, according to the results of his deeds."

JEREMIAH 17:10 NASB

And He said to him, " 'YOU SHALL LOVE THE LORD YOUR GOD WITH ALL YOUR HEART, AND WITH ALL YOUR SOUL, AND WITH ALL YOUR MIND.' "

MATTHEW 22:37 NASB

Keep your heart with all diligence, for out of it spring the issues of life.

PROVERBS 4:23 NKJV

Search me, O God, and know my heart: try me, and know my thoughts: And see if there be any wicked way in me, and lead me in the way everlasting.

PSALM 139:23–24 KJV

Since you have been raised to new life with Christ, set your sights on the realities of heaven, where Christ sits in the place of honor at God's right hand. Think about the things of heaven, not the things of earth. For you died to this life, and your real life is hidden with Christ in God. And when Christ, who is your life, is revealed to the whole world, you will share in all his glory.

COLOSSIANS 3:1–4 NLT

Let the words of my mouth and the meditation of my heart be acceptable in Your sight, O LORD, my strength and my Redeemer.

PSALM 19:14 NKJV

"You will keep him in perfect peace, whose mind is stayed on You, because he trusts in You."

ISAIAH 26:3 NKJV

For *"who has known the mind of the LORD that he may instruct Him?"* But we have the mind of Christ.

1 CORINTHIANS 2:16 NKJV

For the word of God is alive and powerful. It is sharper than the sharpest two-edged sword, cutting between soul and spirit, between joint and marrow. It exposes our innermost thoughts and desires.

HEBREWS 4:12 NLT

Create in me a clean heart, O God, and renew a steadfast spirit within me.

PSALM 51:10 NASB

[Bring] every thought into captivity to the obedience of Christ.

2 CORINTHIANS 10:5 NKJV

"As for you, my son Solomon, know the God of your father, and serve Him with a whole heart and a willing mind; for the LORD searches all hearts, and understands every intent of the thoughts. If you seek Him, He will let you find Him; but if you forsake Him, He will reject you forever."

1 CHRONICLES 28:9 NASB

Let the wicked forsake his way and the evil man his thoughts. Let him turn to the LORD, and he will have mercy on him, and to our God, for he will freely pardon.

ISAIAH 55:7 NIV

Examine me, O LORD, and prove me; try my mind and my heart. For Your lovingkindness is before my eyes, and I have walked in Your truth.

PSALM 26:2–3 NKJV

I will meditate on all Your work and muse on Your deeds.

PSALM 77:12 NASB

For from within, out of the heart of men, proceed evil thoughts, adulteries, fornications, murders, thefts, covetousness, wickedness, deceit, lasciviousness, an evil eye, blasphemy, pride, foolishness: All these evil things come from within, and defile the man.

MARK 7:21–23 KJV

For those who are according to the flesh set their minds on the things of the flesh, but those who are according to the Spirit, the things of the Spirit. For the mind set on the flesh is death, but the mind set on the Spirit is life and peace.

ROMANS 8:5–6 NASB

The peace of God, which surpasses all understanding, will guard your hearts and minds through Christ Jesus.

PHILIPPIANS 4:7 NKJV

When I was a child, I spoke as a child, I understood as a child, I thought as a child; but when I became a man, I put away childish things.

1 CORINTHIANS 13:11 NKJV

Throw off your old sinful nature and your former way of life, which is corrupted by lust and deception. Instead, let the Spirit renew your thoughts and attitudes.

EPHESIANS 4:22–23 NLT

"But seek first His kingdom and His righteousness, and all these things will be added to you."

MATTHEW 6:33 NASB

Thou knowest my downsitting and mine uprising, thou understandest my thought afar off.

PSALM 139:2 KJV

Finally, brothers, whatever is true, whatever is noble, whatever is right, whatever is pure, whatever is lovely, whatever is admirable—if anything is excellent or praiseworthy—think about such things.

PHILIPPIANS 4:8 NIV

UNITY

Now I plead with you, brethren, by the name of our Lord Jesus Christ, that you all speak the same thing, and that there be no divisions among you, but that you be perfectly joined together in the same mind and in the same judgment.

1 CORINTHIANS 1:10 NKJV

Be of the same mind toward one another; do not be haughty in mind, but associate with the lowly. Do not be wise in your own estimation.

ROMANS 12:16 NASB

Make every effort to keep yourselves united in the Spirit,
binding yourselves together with peace.

EPHESIANS 4:3 NLT

Behold, how good and how pleasant it is for brethren to
dwell together in unity!

PSALM 133:1 NKJV

Their hearts may be encouraged, having been knit together in love, and attaining to all the wealth that comes
from the full assurance of understanding, resulting in a
true knowledge of God's mystery, that is, Christ Himself,
in whom are hidden all the treasures of wisdom and
knowledge.

COLOSSIANS 2:2–3 NASB

Do two walk together unless they have agreed to do so?

AMOS 3:3 NIV

And He Himself gave some to be apostles, some prophets,
some evangelists, and some pastors and teachers, for the
equipping of the saints for the work of ministry, for the
edifying of the body of Christ, till we all come to the unity
of the faith and of the knowledge of the Son of God, to a
perfect man, to the measure of the stature of the fullness of
Christ.

EPHESIANS 4:11–13 NKJV

Now may the God who gives perseverance and encouragement grant you to be of the same mind with one another according to Christ Jesus, so that with one accord you may with one voice glorify the God and Father of our Lord Jesus Christ.

ROMANS 15:5–6 NASB

For we were all baptized by one Spirit into one body—whether Jews or Greeks, slave or free—and we were all given the one Spirit to drink.

1 CORINTHIANS 12:13 NIV

Beyond all these things put on love, which is the perfect bond of unity.

COLOSSIANS 3:14 NASB

Therefore if there is any consolation in Christ, if any comfort of love, if any fellowship of the Spirit, if any affection and mercy, fulfill my joy by being like-minded, having the same love, being of one accord, of one mind.

PHILIPPIANS 2:1–2 NKJV

WISDOM

How much better is it to get wisdom than gold! and to get understanding rather to be chosen than silver!

PROVERBS 16:16 KJV

If any of you lacks wisdom, let him ask of God, who gives to all liberally and without reproach, and it will be given to him. But let him ask in faith, with no doubting, for he who doubts is like a wave of the sea driven and tossed by the wind. For let not that man suppose that he will receive anything from the Lord; he is a double-minded man, unstable in all his ways.

JAMES 1:5–8 NKJV

A wise son maketh a glad father: but a foolish son is the heaviness of his mother.

PROVERBS 10:1 KJV

Wisdom and knowledge will be the stability of your times, and the strength of salvation; the fear of the LORD is His treasure.

ISAIAH 33:6 NKJV

Whoever gives heed to instruction prospers, and blessed is he who trusts in the LORD. The wise in heart are called discerning, and pleasant words promote instruction.

PROVERBS 16:20–21 NIV

Those who are wise shall shine like the brightness of the firmament, and those who turn many to righteousness like the stars forever and ever.

DANIEL 12:3 NKJV

Let those who are wise understand these things. Let those with discernment listen carefully. The paths of the LORD are true and right, and righteous people live by walking in them. But in those paths sinners stumble and fall.

HOSEA 14:9 NLT

"Get wisdom! Get understanding! Do not forget, nor turn away from the words of my mouth. Do not forsake her, and she will preserve you; love her, and she will keep you. Wisdom is the principal thing; therefore get wisdom. And in all your getting, get understanding. Exalt her, and she will promote you; she will bring you honor, when you embrace her. She will place on your head an ornament of grace; a crown of glory she will deliver to you." Hear, my son, and receive my sayings, and the years of your life will be many. I have taught you in the way of wisdom; I have led you in right paths. When you walk, your steps will not be hindered, and when you run, you will not stumble. Take firm hold of instruction, do not let go; keep her, for she is your life.

PROVERBS 4:5–13 NKJV

The teaching of the wise is a fountain of life, to turn aside from the snares of death. Good understanding produces favor, but the way of the treacherous is hard.

PROVERBS 13:14–15 NASB

For the report of your obedience has reached to all; therefore I am rejoicing over you, but I want you to be wise in what is good and innocent in what is evil.

ROMANS 16:19 NASB

"Therefore everyone who hears these words of Mine and acts on them, may be compared to a wise man who built his house on the rock. And the rain fell, and the floods came, and the winds blew and slammed against that house; and yet it did not fall, for it had been founded on the rock."

MATTHEW 7:24–25 NASB

Love wisdom like a sister; make insight a beloved member of your family.

PROVERBS 7:4 NLT

Who is wise? Let him give heed to these things, and consider the lovingkindnesses of the LORD.

PSALM 107:43 NASB

"I, wisdom, dwell together with prudence; I possess knowledge and discretion."

PROVERBS 8:12 NIV

He who keeps his command will experience nothing harmful; and a wise man's heart discerns both time and judgment.

ECCLESIASTES 8:5 NKJV

But if any of you lacks wisdom, let him ask of God, who gives to all generously and without reproach, and it will be given to him.

JAMES 1:5 NASB

However, we speak wisdom among those who are mature, yet not the wisdom of this age, nor of the rulers of this age, who are coming to nothing. But we speak the wisdom of God in a mystery, the hidden wisdom which God ordained before the ages for our glory, which none of the rulers of this age knew; for had they known, they would not have crucified the Lord of glory.

1 CORINTHIANS 2:6–8 NKJV

Who is a wise man and endued with knowledge among you? let him shew out of a good conversation his works with meekness of wisdom. But if ye have bitter envying and strife in your hearts, glory not, and lie not against the truth. This wisdom descendeth not from above, but is earthly, sensual, devilish. . . . But the wisdom that is from above is first pure, then peaceable, gentle, and easy to be intreated, full of mercy and good fruits, without partiality, and without hypocrisy.

JAMES 3:13–15, 17 KJV

WITNESSING

Yet for this reason I found mercy, so that in me as the foremost, Jesus Christ might demonstrate His perfect patience as an example for those who would believe in Him for eternal life.

1 TIMOTHY 1:16 NASB

"You are the light of the world. A city on a hill cannot be hidden. Neither do people light a lamp and put it under a bowl. Instead they put it on its stand, and it gives light to everyone in the house. In the same way, let your light shine before men, that they may see your good deeds and praise your Father in heaven."

MATTHEW 5:14–16 NIV

And have no fellowship with the unfruitful works of darkness, but rather expose them. For it is shameful even to speak of those things which are done by them in secret. But all things that are exposed are made manifest by the light, for whatever makes manifest is light.

EPHESIANS 5:11–13 NKJV

Therefore do not be ashamed of the testimony of our Lord, nor of me His prisoner, but share with me in the sufferings for the gospel according to the power of God.

2 TIMOTHY 1:8 NKJV

My brethren, if any among you strays from the truth and one turns him back, let him know that he who turns a sinner from the error of his way will save his soul from death and will cover a multitude of sins.

JAMES 5:19–20 NASB

Rescuing you from the Jewish people and from the Gentiles, to whom I am sending you, to open their eyes so that they may turn from darkness to light and from the dominion of Satan to God, that they may receive forgiveness of sins and an inheritance among those who have been sanctified by faith in Me.

ACTS 26:17–18 NASB

Preach the word! Be ready in season and out of season. Convince, rebuke, exhort, with all longsuffering and teaching.

2 TIMOTHY 4:2 NKJV

But in your hearts set apart Christ as Lord. Always be prepared to give an answer to everyone who asks you to give the reason for the hope that you have. But do this with gentleness and respect.

1 PETER 3:15 NIV

Let the redeemed of the LORD say so, whom He has redeemed from the hand of the adversary.

PSALM 107:2 NASB

WORSHIP

And Jesus answered and said to him, "Get behind Me, Satan! For it is written, '*You shall worship the LORD your God, and Him only you shall serve.*'"

LUKE 4:8 NKJV

"Do not follow other gods to serve and worship them; do not provoke me to anger with what your hands have made. Then I will not harm you."

JEREMIAH 25:6 NIV

"But an hour is coming, and now is, when the true worshipers will worship the Father in spirit and truth; for such people the Father seeks to be His worshipers. God is spirit, and those who worship Him must worship in spirit and truth."

JOHN 4:23–24 NASB

All the nations you made will come and bow before you, Lord; they will praise your holy name.

PSALM 86:9 NLT

"Then the sovereignty, the dominion and the greatness of all the kingdoms under the whole heaven will be given to the people of the saints of the Highest One; His kingdom will be an everlasting kingdom, and all the dominions will serve and obey Him."

DANIEL 7:27 NASB

Then I saw another angel flying in the midst of heaven, having the everlasting gospel to preach to those who dwell on the earth—to every nation, tribe, tongue, and people— saying with a loud voice, "Fear God and give glory to Him, for the hour of His judgment has come; and worship Him who made heaven and earth, the sea and springs of water."

REVELATION 14:6–7 NKJV

"You alone are the LORD. You have made the heavens, the heaven of heavens with all their host, the earth and all that is on it, the seas and all that is in them. You give life to all of them and the heavenly host bows down before You."

NEHEMIAH 9:6 NASB

"Who shall not fear You, O Lord, and glorify Your name? For You alone are holy. For all nations shall come and worship before You, for Your judgments have been manifested."

REVELATION 15:4 NKJV

Therefore, since we receive a kingdom which cannot be shaken, let us show gratitude, by which we may offer to God an acceptable service with reverence and awe.

HEBREWS 12:28 NASB

I beseech you therefore, brethren, by the mercies of God, that ye present your bodies a living sacrifice, holy, acceptable unto God, which is your reasonable service.

ROMANS 12:1 KJV

"But the LORD your God you shall fear; and He will deliver you from the hand of all your enemies."

2 KINGS 17:39 NKJV

Ascribe to the LORD the glory due His name; bring an offering, and come before Him; worship the LORD in holy array.

1 CHRONICLES 16:29 NASB

Serve the LORD with gladness: come before his presence with singing.

PSALM 100:2 KJV

Come, let us worship and bow down. Let us kneel before the LORD our maker.

PSALM 95:6 NLT